BRAVEY

BRAVEY

ADAPTED FOR YOUNG READERS

CHASING DREAMS, BEFRIENDING PAIN, AND OTHER BIG IDEAS

ALEXI PAPPAS

FOREWORD BY MAYA HAWKE

Delacorte Press

Text copyright © 2023 by Alexi Pappas
Foreword copyright © 2023 by Maya Hawke
Jacket art copyright © 2023 by Steffi Walthall
Interior art used under license from Shutterstock

This work is based on *Bravey: Chasing Dreams, Befriending Pain, and Other Big Ideas,* copyright © 2021 by Alexi Pappas. Originally published in hardcover by The Dial Press, an imprint of Random House, a division of Penguin Random House LLC, New York, in 2021.

Delacorte Press is a registered trademark and the colophon is a trademark of Penguin Random House LLC.

"My Pal, Pain" was originally published in a different form in *Lenny Letter,* August 17, 2016.

Visit us on the Web! GetUnderlined.com

Educators and librarians, for a variety of teaching tools, visit us at RHTeachersLibrarians.com

Library of Congress Cataloging-in-Publication Data
Names: Pappas, Alexi, author.
Title: Bravey : chasing dreams, befriending pain, and other big ideas / Alexi Pappas ; foreword by Maya Hawke.
Description: First edition. | New York : Delacorte Press, 2023. | "Adapted for young readers." | Audience: Ages 10 up | Summary: "Olympic runner, actress, filmmaker, and writer Alexi Pappas shares the touchstone moments in her life that helped her learn about confidence and self-reliance, compassion and forgiveness, and loss and hope. Adapted for young readers from Bravey: Chasing Dreams, Befriending Pain, and Other Big Ideas (The Dial Press; 2021)" —Provided by publisher.
Identifiers: LCCN 2022055406 (print) | LCCN 2022055407 (ebook) | ISBN 978-0-593-56274-1 (hardcover) | ISBN 978-0-593-56276-5 (ebook) | ISBN 978-0-593-56277-2 (paperback)
Subjects: LCSH: Pappas, Alexi—Juvenile literature. | Runners (Sports)—United States—Biography—Juvenile literature. | Women runners—United States—Biography—Juvenile literature. | Women Olympic athletes—Greece—Biography—Juvenile literature. | Women motion picture producers and directors—United States—Biography—Juvenile literature. | Children of suicide victims—United States—Biography—Juvenile literature. | Greek Americans—Biography—Juvenile literature. | Courage—Juvenile literature. | Conduct of life—Juvenile literature.
Classification: LCC GV1061.15.P37 A3 2023 (print) | LCC GV1061.15.P37 (ebook) | DDC 796.42092 [B]—dc23/eng/20230117

The text of this book is set in 11.5-point Utopia Std.
Interior design by Michelle Crowe

Printed in the United States of America
10 9 8 7 6 5 4 3 2 1
First Edition

This book is for the Braveys.

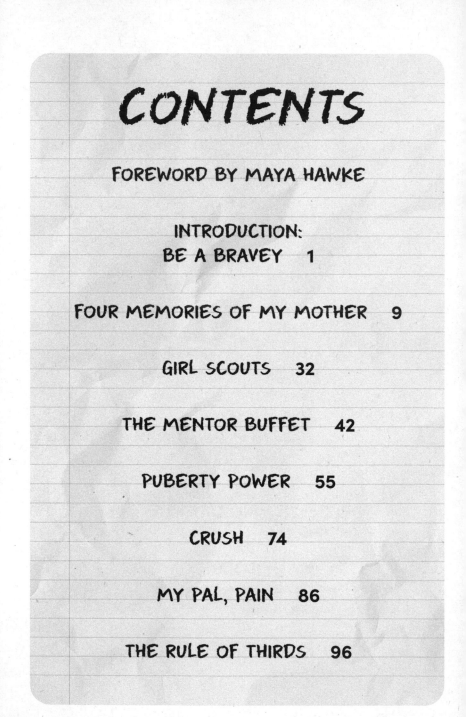

CONTENTS

FOREWORD BY MAYA HAWKE

When I first went to acting school, I was unpleasantly surprised to find it was more like gym class than anything else. I ate a big breakfast before my first "movement" class and I fully threw up my BLT in a trash can in the hallway halfway through. We were rolling around on the floor doing jumping jacks and tai chi and I was . . . angry about it, to say the least. During an open forum where students could talk about our experiences, I raised my hand and openly critiqued the curriculum. "I came here to study, not to exercise!" I said. (Ew gross I hate 18 year old me.)

I was never an athletic kid. I didn't do sports at all when I was growing up. In the fourth grade I almost managed to FAIL gym, so I had to run a mile during the last week of school and I hated every single one of the twenty-five minutes it took me. I saw my body as a rickety old car I had to use in order to move my brain from one place to another. I only ever thought about my body in terms of what it looked like from the outside to other people, never what it felt like to live in it. It was always about getting smaller, never about getting stronger or faster or more flexible. My body was more of a liability than a joy.

So as a freshman in acting school, I couldn't care less about movement class. I didn't see any connection between movement and learning my craft. But then my favorite teacher said something that really changed my life: "Maya, when your shoulders are as open and curious as your mind, I will talk to you about rigorous text analysis. Until then, I think you should refrain from asking any more questions."

"How do I get curious shoulders?" I thought. *"What does that even mean?"*

At first I just pretended to take his advice. I kept my head down and threw myself into my movement classes and tried not to be embarrassed about how much worse I was than the other students. But little by little, something started to change. I stopped obsessing over food. I actually wanted to eat because I needed energy to learn the things I was trying to learn. I stopped looking in the mirror as much and forgot to suck in my stomach. I started sleeping better and breathing more deeply and little by little I stopped comparing myself to the other students and started dancing with them.

I got out of my own head and into my own body.

And what can I say . . . my shoulders got curious. And— CRAZY!!!—my acting got better. When I first started acting, I could only play characters who were uncomfortable in their body like me (and if you've seen Stranger Things, you know I still have that in my wheelhouse). But in getting to know my body in this new way, I found I could access other characters too: steady people, sturdy people, angry people, slow people, heavy people, frail people, powerful people. I got curious about my body and its movement, and that gave me access to parts of my heart and mind I had never seen before. Not only could I access more of myself onstage, I could access more of myself in my own life. Finding the connective tissue between my mind and body, simply put, opened up possibilities.

And that's what every single day of my silly stupid little life game is all about. Discovering possibilities. Getting interested in all the different and amazing ways there are to be strong:

I can walk with a limp and spit like a cowboy in a baggy suit,
I can wear a corset and ball gown,
I have been inside a room while a baby was being born,

I have tried to climb a mountain and knit a sweater.
I can drag my feet and spin my hips and . . . I can run.

I never really tried running until I read *Bravey,* but now, when I'm feeling sad or stressed or overwhelmed I put my headphones on and I run until I break a sweat. I don't run away from my tough feelings, I run towards them. I run them from my head into my shoulders and down my spine. I run my feelings all the way to my fingertips and toes. I sweat them out and shower them off.

I run on my constant hunt for more possibilities.

I believe that no matter who you are or how you want to exist in school or what you want to be when you grow up, we all benefit from possibilities; from not getting stuck in one way of being . . . as the smart girl or the fast girl or the annoying girl or the sad girl. I have been all those girls in the last hour—and I think (I hope) that the willingness to be all those people makes me a brave girl. I am a Bravey.

Never in a million years would I have thought I'd like running. Certainly, the Maya from fourth grade gym class would never believe it. In absolutely no way is this book propaganda to get kids moving, but reading about the feelings of confidence and capability that Alexi got from putting one foot in front of the other inspired me to try the same.

This book is about so much more than running. It is about growing up.

Alexi has struggled with challenges and overcome them in ways I did not expect and could not see from the outside.

My struggle was with words.

I am dyslexic—and as many of you probably know, if you can find a good teacher who knows the right ways to teach you it's no big deal, but it feels like a *big deal* when you are in the third grade and they call on you to read out loud in class and you stumble on the word *"bird."* I was desperate to prove I wasn't an ignoramus so reading and writing became my obsession . . . loving it took over my identity as a teenager with as much ferocity as hating it did when I was in lower school.

Even though I still lean toward audio books over handheld books (I read *Bravey* on audio the first time), my dyslexia is what helped me gravitate toward plays and movies . . . books that had literally flown off the page. I found a way to turn a weakness into a window. In the end it helped guide me toward what would be the focus and passion of my life.

Through my friendship with Alexi, I was surprised to learn that even though Alexi and I have grown up so differently and faced different challenges, the feeling of overcoming our personal hurdles with whatever tools we had was very similar. The outside is different, but the inside feels the same.

I have learned how Alexi has developed tools and mental approaches to overcoming her hurdles. You will learn about those in this book. And even though your hurdles might be different from Alexi's, just like mine were, I know you'll feel seen and inspired by reading *Bravey*, just like I was.

I spent so long feeling trapped by my body, and now my body and I are on the same team. We explore together, learn together, grow together, change together. And to me that's what being a Bravey is all about. Becoming friends with yourself.

dear boy in middle school who told me
i look like a "before" picture:

i'm not mad anymore. you are brilliant.
i am always becoming a better me.

INTRODUCTION

BE A BRAVEY

My earliest memory of running was in the first grade when a boy in my class made fun of my best friend, and I not only chased him down but caught him and stabbed him with a pencil to make sure he knew I wasn't messing around. I took the bus to school every morning, and I loved to wait until the bus was approaching my stop, then take off and try to outrun it to the next stop. If I couldn't outrun the bus I'd be late to school, and that was on me. In middle school I channeled my athletic ability in a more productive way: the track team. Organized chasing. We had weekly meets at the local high school dirt track, which was very exciting to us middle-schoolers. The meets were coed, and I won them all. I liked the feeling of winning. It made me feel like I mattered. All I've ever wanted in my life is to matter.

* * *

I was born in Berkeley, California, and I grew up in a safe slice of suburbia outside of San Francisco with my remarkable father and loving older brother. With our nearest extended family thousands of miles away on the East Coast, the three of us were a tight unit, making our own rules and our own way in the world. But despite the privilege and security of my upbringing, my bright future was not guaranteed. My first five years of life coincided with my mom's last. Shortly after I came into the world, my mom became so mentally ill that she had to be hospitalized. For all I know, I was the last straw that sent her over the edge. I am always saddened by the sense that I came at just the wrong time.

She was diagnosed as bipolar with manic depression, and after developing an addiction to pain pills originally prescribed to treat a back injury due to pregnancy complications, she became suicidal—unsuccessfully at first and then, eventually, successfully. But my mom succeeded in other things long before she succeeded at suicide. She was an accomplished athlete and one of the first female software consultants at her company. What I now understand is that a successful person can be successful in anything, the good and the bad. This is both empowering and heartbreaking.

Living with my mom for the first five years of my childhood forced me to learn how to survive in a different way. I had an awareness of just how extreme life could be. Like all kids, the thing I wanted most in the world was attention. But when you're a toddler and the person throwing temper tantrums in your house is your mom instead of you, attention is hard to come by. It was easy to feel like I didn't matter.

When I saw how my dad and the parade of doctors were always crowding around my mom and paying attention to her, my four-year-old brain could only think: Why don't people pay attention to *me* like that? It wasn't that my dad didn't want to give me all the attention in the world, it was just that he couldn't. All of my early memories, even the happy ones, are tinted with this feeling that I'm the least interesting thing in the room.

Mattering taunted me because it felt like it was not for me. I remember feeling desperate to do whatever it took to get the attention I craved. And so I decided that I would need to become the most interesting thing in the room. I decided that even though I didn't matter enough for my mom to choose to stay with me, I would matter to everyone else. I would become great. I translated my internal desires into external effort. I would learn, in time, how painful and unsustainable it is to be fueled by trauma like this. But I am where I am because of it.

3

In those middle school years, whether I won a race or not was purely a question of how hard I could push myself. It was a contest of me versus my own pain tolerance. This is why I love to run. Because it is a way for me to push on and explore the outermost limits of myself, mentally and physically, in a way that is fundamentally good. That basic principle has held true throughout my running career, from my time as a young natural to when I was the worst on my college team all the way up to competing in the Olympics. The same dynamic applies to my creative pursuits: How much pain, how much uncertainty, how much discomfort am I brave enough to endure before I give up? Being brave is the best way to survive, and I've always been about survival. As I grew into a decorated college athlete and then into an Olympian (with some major ups and downs along the way), I began to attract a modest but loyal following of younger athletes on social media. However small my audience was at first, I was keenly aware that being a role model is a privilege and a responsibility. When I was growing up, I sought out female role models shamelessly, watched them wide-eyed, and leaned on them hard. The best tools are the ones you have with you, not the ones you don't, and as a motherless daughter I have always been very forthcoming about my desire for mentorship. I idolized Mia Hamm and I mailed fan letters to the Spice Girls; the girls on the Cal Berkeley women's soccer team were like gods to me. I looked up to my friends' mothers and my college professors, and then, as I began my running career and making movies, I looked up to Olympians and artists.

I knew there would be kids, much like the little girl I had once been, who would pore over every word I posted and try their best to imitate me. I didn't want them trying to replicate my hundred-plus-miles-a-week training regimen; I wanted to give them something they could healthily adopt as their own. So instead of posting workout splits, I posted poems.

The poems were whimsical, silly thoughts, sometimes from the perspective of a runner but just as often from the perspective of two shoes in love or a trail that misses the runner after she's gone. One night, before a particularly daunting workout, I typed out this poem:

> run like a bravey
> sleep like a baby
> dream like a crazy
> replace can't with maybe

It was the first time I used the word *bravey,* and it stuck. It became the label for a mini-movement, a self-identifier for those who are willing to chase their dreams even though it can be intimidating and scary. It celebrates the choice to pursue a goal and even relishes the pain that comes with effort. There is nobility to it; it's something to be celebrated.

Growing up, I chased specific labels: strong, fierce, fast, funny, pretty. But all of those labels were *outward facing*—they described an energy you project into the world. Being a bravey is different. It's *inward facing,* a choice you make about your relationship with yourself. We all have dreams that we're chasing, however big or small, and we can all decide to be brave enough to give ourselves a chance. I think that's why the term resonated with so many people: Anyone can be a bravey, and the permutations of what that means are infinite. It's a switch you flip in your mind.

* * *

In writing a book about chasing dreams, I am, in fact, chasing one of my dreams: to write something that I know will *matter,* to you and to me. Chasing a dream is a never-ending negotiation, as in, you have to keep navigating, pivoting, adapting, and persisting. It's a process that unfolds continually and never in a straight line.

This book is about glamorous things like going to the Olympics and making movies, and it's also about difficult things like suicide and depression and puberty. For every fun moment of victory in this book, there are uncomfortable and humiliating moments, too. I am the sum of all of them. I want to show you the whole picture, the bad pain and the good pain. This book is gore and glory. This book is about making a life, not just living a life. By sharing my story so far, I can show you what being a bravey means to me. In turn, you can decide what being a bravey means to you.

good thing i didn't accomplish all my goals yet
because then what would i do tomorrow?

FOUR MEMORIES OF
MY MOTHER

I used to feed the ducks that lived in the lagoon behind our house. My dad went with me sometimes, but most often I went alone—the lagoon bordered our back-yard and it was easy for me to slip away. My favorite day to feed the ducks was Saturday, which was when moms and daughters were out in force. I'm sure other people were out there, too, but I have always cared most about moms and daughters.

Moms were aliens to me, foreign creatures I could only see outside of my home. I'd observe them from my vantage point atop a pile of wood chips as they walked down the bike path along the lagoon's edge. Obsessively watching those women was a compulsion stronger than being glued to Saturday-morning cartoons.

The moms would always walk with a bag of stale

bread in one hand and their daughter's small hand in the other. I so badly wanted to experience that feeling of having my hand held by a woman who was walking half a step ahead of me. Wherever she was going, we'd head there together. A little girl's understanding of the world revolves around her mother, but I could only ever watch from afar. Observing the moms and daughters felt like looking at the moon through a telescope: I could see it was there, but *I* was not there and never could be. Can you miss something you never had?

I liked to watch how the moms talked to other moms, acting as translators if their kids wanted to add anything to the conversation, always so understanding of each other, nodding and smiling and laughing. I thought maybe my mom didn't realize she could have gone to the park to find people to talk to.

Today, I imagine all little kids as potatoes, wondrous nuggets of raw potential just waiting to be shaped by their mom-chefs. Whether your mom tenderly styles you into a Hasselback dish, tosses you in the microwave, or is totally absent, she is going to affect you. My mother took her own life before there was much time for her to shape me into anything. I was four years old, almost five. The greatest legacy she left me was her suicide. I try to imagine what it feels like to be washed, dried, peeled—to be turned over under warm water, then pushed gently into an oven and checked on every now and again. But it is another thing entirely to never be touched at all; to be left alone in the cabinet to sprout eyes and fend for yourself.

* * *

Before she died, my mother was in and out of my life like a jack-in-the-box. By the time I was four years old I knew she was sick, I just didn't understand quite what that meant. At that age, "sick" meant a sneeze or maybe an ear infection. It had easy-to-spot symptoms and was cured by taking gooey sweet red medicine. But none of that applied to my mother's mental illness. Depression is an invisible injury. Back then people generally didn't understand that depression is an injury like any other. Depression is something that you *have,* not something that you *are.* The stigma around depression begins with the way we talk about it and the way we label it. But I didn't understand this as a kid. I was looking for sneezes, but all I saw were screams.

My mother had to be kept in a special place, locked up, safe from herself. But even there she was not entirely safe. According to her medical reports, she once lit her room and herself on fire. The orderlies caught her and she did not die that day. What do you need to feel inside to light yourself on fire? Do you feel fire inside that you need to get out, or do you feel nothing inside and so maybe lighting your hospital bed on fire and lying down in it is the only thing that can make you feel something? I was brought to visit her the way you'd visit someone in jail, in a highly controlled and scheduled way, but I don't remember anything other than the sterile white walls and fluorescent lights.

My mother was deeply mysterious to me. In my mind's eye she was very tall, which is funny because I later learned she was well under five feet. I'm actually much taller now than she was, but even so, in all of my imagined scenarios where I meet her again she is still somehow taller than me. She used to wear swooshy nylon sweat suits with matching pants and a jacket. I cannot remember her ever wearing anything but these matching sweat suits. When I wear matching sweat suits now, it is a secret nod to her.

Sometimes my mother was allowed to come home. This was a highly anticipated event in my family. It meant she had demonstrated enough outward-facing progress to be released from the asylum. Even as a toddler I could tell it was a very big deal. It's a special occasion! But when my mother came home it never felt like she belonged there. I remember knowing *in theory* how moms and daughters were supposed to embrace and feel at ease with each other, but I was never able to actually achieve this with my mother. I don't remember ever hugging her. I'm sure she sensed this awkwardness, too, which must have made it even harder for her to come home—especially when it meant coming home to my brother and me, two little potatoes who were growing and transforming wildly, always one step more evolved than the last time she saw us. I imagine that she must have felt increasingly alienated from us and maybe even started thinking that it would be better if she were gone.

Even though her goal with suicide might have been to disappear, there are things about her I will never be able to forget. I have four memories of my mother, and three of them are bad. They sit in the back of my mind all the time, like a lady on a green velvet chaise longue who mostly blends into the background but will sometimes wink and wave at me to get my attention. There is a part of me that likes that at least she is still something, even if I remember she is there at all the wrong times. I am learning, slowly, to simply wave back.

* * *

In my earliest memory of my mother, she's leaning against the doorframe of the office in our old house wearing a red edition of the nylon sweat suit and smoking a cigarette. I still think of her anytime I smell cigarette smoke. My dad never told her not to smoke inside the house, even though I could see it bothered him. I figured that she was allowed because she was special. She stood in the doorway staring into nowhere, totally motionless save for the cigarette. Her hair, which was short and curly, absorbed the smoke around her. She looked like a movie poster to me, grainy and glamorous and ethereal, not all the way there. People have a certain demeanor when they're smoking cigarettes. Their hands are occupied and so is their mouth; they are not able to hold your hand or kiss you.

My mother and I were home alone—my dad tried to be there to supervise as much as he could, but sometimes he had to leave. This was always a roll of the dice for him, since he never knew what she was going to do next, ever. Her behavior ranged from compulsively buying things, like several life-size wooden parrot statuettes that she hung throughout the house, to crashing our family's minivan (possibly on purpose). Thankfully, I was not in the car when she wrecked it, but they found the toddler car seat dangling upside down because it had not been secured properly. She was like a natural disaster and my dad was on alert all the time, never sure when her next episode was coming and how severe it would be—all the while balancing a full-time job, taking care of my brother and me, and managing my mom's care while keeping her condition a secret. Her stays at home always ended abruptly with her needing to be committed to some hospital, whether it was the psych ward or a rehab clinic or I don't know where else.

My mother was mesmerizing to me. I watched her smoke her cigarette and then I walked up next to her, almost close enough to touch her.

Almost close enough to feel the swooshy nylon against my skin. And then, all of a sudden, she came to life. She looked down at me as though I were a problem she didn't quite know how to solve. It wasn't mean but it wasn't nice. It was almost curious. She paused, took a puff of her cigarette, and then did something I don't remember her ever having done before: She reached her arm out to me. The caramel-brown mouthpiece was inches from my lips, and just out of focus was the bright hot point with smoke tendrils curling up to the ceiling. I understood she was offering me a puff. She didn't make a big deal of holding the cigarette in front of my mouth. It felt casual, almost like an accident—except it wasn't. I immediately felt special. The rules did not apply to us. I was her daughter and she was sharing something with me that had touched her lips and soon would touch mine. I felt like I was included in an exclusive thing that I had only ever seen her doing alone.

She held the cigarette to my mouth and I did what I

had seen her do. I inhaled shyly, watching her as I did. The smoke was curiously harsh, like nothing I'd ever tasted before. I was used to soft things like chocolate milk and macaroni and cheese. I sensed that what was happening was not normal, that we were breaking a rule, but still I did it. I wanted her to love me more than I wanted to be good. I wanted her to include me. Who behaves crazier, a mentally ill person or a four-year-old who desperately wants her mother's love? When the most important person in your life is floating away like a ghost, you seize any opportunity you can to feel a connection with her. So of course I smoked the cigarette, even though I knew that smoking was B-A-D bad.

* * *

One of the other times they let my mother come home, I was on the staircase with my knees between the balusters and she was in the kitchen wearing her swooshy sweat suit like always, this time in turquoise. She was screaming at the top of her lungs about I don't know what, I just remember that she looked like a demon in the body of a giant Barbie doll with the kind of bird's-nest hair your Barbie gets when you brush it too much. She was yelling at my dad, who was on the other side of the doorway just out of sight. He never yelled back, not once. I remember that more than feeling scared, I was curious. How could someone yell so loudly and channel so much anger? Each shout built momentum like a snowball that keeps gathering more of itself as it rolls downhill and nothing can stop the avalanche it becomes.

I was hungry and wanted cereal but I didn't dare go down to the screaming zone. So I just stared at my mother from my staircase perch. I was frustrated. When a little kid is hungry it is her right to demand attention until the hunger is solved. But with my mom around, I had to be a quiet pair of eyes with no needs. Most young kids are only concerned with how the world makes *them* feel, but I saw the world as a place I needed to navigate in a more thoughtful way. To me, it felt more sad than unfair. Because as I watched my mom in that moment, throwing a tantrum and screaming, I realized, *she could not handle herself.* And I felt, for the first time in my life, sad for another human being. And when you feel sad for someone it's very hard to resent them, even if they're hurting you. But it's also impossible to admire and look up to someone you feel sorry for.

My dad taught me to view my mom with compassion. He explained that she wasn't the boss of herself. I knew that also meant that she was not the boss of me. How could she be? A role model is supposed to be someone who knows more than you, someone who is a step *beyond where you are.* My mother was not a step beyond. She was not anywhere in my vicinity. Even though I was curious about what it would feel like to receive love and attention and affection and guidance from her, at the same time, I knew she wasn't going to be able to do that for me. Nor was she someone to imitate. I was still desperately curious about her, but I knew it was best not to get too close. And this made me feel different from other little girls and their moms, orbiting each other like a planet and its moon as they walked down the bike path behind my house to feed the ducks. I saw then that I was going to have to be my own planet, or maybe an asteroid floating free.

* * *

The third memory of my mother is violent and terrifying and I try not to think of it very often. It must have happened sometime after we shared the cigarette. I remember going into my parents' room unannounced, as kids often do. The bedroom light was off but the bathroom light was on. My parents' bathroom had those round bulbs that make you look like a movie star, and the light spilled out into the dark bedroom, beckoning me to investigate. I crept forward . . . and there, in the mirror above the sink, I saw my mother glamorously illuminated. She was making a back-and-forth motion with one arm and she was very focused, with her attention completely centered on what she was doing. I tiptoed closer and saw that she was gripping a mean-looking metal saw with a wooden handle and a long triangular blade with big rusty teeth and using it to harm herself. There was plenty of blood. This was and still is the most violent and sad thing I have ever seen. The older I get, the sadder this memory makes me—not for me, but for her.

I knew that what I was seeing wasn't right. My mom wasn't showing any signs of pain, which was confusing to me because I knew that blood meant *pain*. I spent a lot of time playing outside and I'd taken my share of bad falls. When you bled, it meant you were hurt and then you cried. So why wasn't my mom crying? I stood motionless, processing. I couldn't look away.

Then she turned around and saw me. She caught me catching her. Who was in bigger trouble? I knew I was seeing something I shouldn't and I wondered what kind of trouble I would be in for walking in on this. She stopped sawing for a moment but she didn't seem upset that I was there. She didn't even seem surprised. I can't remember *ever* seeing her act surprised, which is a quality I now associate with a sane person—the capacity for surprise. My mom and I have the same thick eyebrows and hers were not curved up in astonishment, angled down in anger, or drooping sideways with sadness. They were completely flat.

"What are you doing?" I asked. I knew what she was doing, but I also didn't know what she was *doing*.

"Don't tell your father," she replied, holding a flat stare for a beat before returning to her task.

The gears in my head whirred. My mother gave me an order, but even as a four-and-a-half-year-old, my instincts told me this was not right. So I ran. I used my legs intentionally and purposefully for the very first time to save my mom's life. I ran down the hall and found my dad. What's strange is that I cannot remember what happened after that, not even the moment I found my dad. I only know I was a big fat tattletale and she didn't die that day, so I must have found him in time. My dad has always been there when I needed him.

After she was taken to the hospital, I tried to make sense of what I had seen. My dad never talked to me about this experience. Maybe he was hoping it would fade on its own like a bruise. It didn't fade and we never talked about it. After you've experienced something unspeakable, how can you possibly make sense of it? The only point of reference I had was from Saturday-morning cartoons. There is a Looney Tunes trope where Bugs Bunny or Yosemite Sam or the Big Bad Wolf will use a saw—the same kind of wood-handled, triangular saw my mom used—to sabotage another character in some mischievous way. I remember the saw made an appearance at least once in every episode. So when I recognized the same cartoon saw in my mom's hand, my four-year-old mind experienced a reality warp where the line between the cartoon world and the real world was shattered. If things that happen in the cartoon world can happen in real life, I reasoned, then *anything is possible.* I understood that of course cartoons were not real, but my mind stretched in both directions like Silly Putty: if the most unimaginably *terrible* things are possible, like your mother hurting herself in front of you, then the most magically *good* things must also be possible, like, well, *anything.* That day, I saved her life, but I also had to save my own. I chose optimism. Life never serves you the lessons you need in the way you might imagine you'd receive them, but the lessons are nonetheless there, even if they are embedded in blood.

* * *

I have one good memory of my mother that I hold on to. It begins and ends in about four seconds, like a dream you try to keep when you first wake up but it inevitably slips away as the day sets in. In the memory, I'm on the path that leads from our house to the lagoon where kids feed the ducks and I am riding my two-wheeler bike for the first time. As I pedal, I look back over my shoulder and I see my mother standing in the doorframe of our house watching me. She is actually *watching me*! She wears a sweat suit like always and she's smoking a cigarette, but she is *paying attention to me*. The feeling of being watched is the next best thing to being touched. It's like sunlight on your skin, as though the person watching you is giving you some part of themselves by way of their eyes. The memory stops when I look back and see her. I don't really know what happened after that moment—I don't know if I fell down, or if she turned and went back inside, or if I just rode away. What is important is the memory of her eyes on me. My dad later confirmed that my mother did indeed teach me how to ride a bike, so now in my mind I've added a part at the beginning where she pushes me in a grand send-off, hands hovering attentively over my shoulders to catch me if I fall. And even though I don't know if that part is true, I've imagined it so many times that it *feels* true. I use my imagination for self-care in this way. My imagination comforts and nurtures me in moments of confusion, bullying, self-consciousness, and generally feeling like life is the hardest thing ever.

My imagination also lifts me. I often imagine things into existence until I don't know the difference between what is real and what isn't, what doesn't exist and what *could* exist if I believe it hard enough. I've visualized so many wonderful things into reality for myself. Becoming an Olympian took an extraordinary amount of hard work, but all it started with my belief that it could be true. Imagination, at the very least, brings us joy; at the very most, it empowers us to suspend disbelief and chase the impossible. Imagining things into existence is a super-power. The only sad part is that there will always be one thing I can never imagine into existence: having my mom back. Whenever I think of her, I always see her in one of those same four memories, repeating her actions endlessly in a loop like an automaton at Disney World. I've tried to make her do things like pour me cereal, but I can't. I cannot imagine her outside these very specific and brief memories. I cannot have her in those ways. But anything else is fair game.

* * *

One day my mother finally got away and did the thing she was trying to do. It was the middle of the night and we were all asleep. We've always been heavy sleepers in my family. But my dad woke up and realized she was gone, and when he searched the house he found blood on the floor of the downstairs bathroom. He called the security guards that patrolled our island city and they found her body among the trees along the lagoon's edge, right where everyone feeds the ducks, next to the path where she taught me to ride my bike.

What gets me the most is that after she fatally cut herself, my mother made one last decision: she used her remaining strength to get out of the house where we were all asleep and go someplace to die where we wouldn't find her body. This small fact makes all the difference in the world. I like to believe that even though she was gripped by anguish so severe that she wanted to die, her final thoughts were of protecting my dad, my brother, and me. For my mother, this gesture was as thoughtful as she could have been. It makes me so grateful and also so sad. I hold on to this thoughtfulness as tightly as I would have held on to her if I could.

* * *

Did you ever realize *funeral* has the word *fun* in it? The cemetery where we buried my mom was surrounded by these irresistible hills, and I remember my brother, Louis, and I ran up and down the grassy slopes having a grand time, until I tried to chase Louis down a particularly steep slope in my patent leather slippers and fell down and cried for the first and only time that day. Younger siblings engage themselves in the self-inflicted torture of trying to keep up with their older siblings, for which they pay dearly in the form of tears. There were even ducks nearby, like the lagoon in our neighborhood. But here there were no moms and daughters out for strolls, just crying people. I wore a pretty dress that got very dirty and a single shiny earring. Before the funeral I had begged my dad to take me to get my ears pierced, but after one ear I decided it hurt too much and ran out of the store before they could finish the job. I didn't look like some kids do when they get all dressed up, like a miniature version of an adult. I looked very much like a kid.

The congregation around my mother's grave was the largest group of people I'd ever seen gathered on account of one person. Before my mom died, it was easier to keep her condition quiet. Back then mental illness wasn't handled openly with flowers and get-well cards like there might have been if she had been sick with a different disease. Her side of the family was out of the picture, both before and after her death—when she was living they refused to acknowledge she was sick, and when she died nobody from her family even came to the funeral, except for her father—and so my dad was left on his own throughout my mom's illness. My mother's depression was easy to keep out of sight. At the time, I didn't know she had taken her own life. I thought she had died from cigarettes. Nobody corrected my assumption until seventh grade, when my best friend told me the truth about how she died. For everyone else, it was easier to hide the truth of my mom's suicide than to face it and understand it.

In my family, we did not want to talk about the big stuff, the messy stuff. We hardly ever talked about our feelings. Instead, we took action: If you are tired, you sleep. If you are sad, you cry. If you are angry, you throw a temper tantrum or, in my brother's case, you beat up your little sister. But talking about the sad feelings that made you cry or the mad feelings that made you lose control, that was just not done. If I was upset, I cried until all the rage was gone while my dad said, "I know, I know, I'm sorry," as if these feelings were just waves that I needed to ride out. Trying to reason with my feelings would be as useless as a sailor trying to negotiate with the waves. Better to ride them out when they come. Maybe my dad felt that it was too hard to engage with the emotions that take hold of two young kids whose mom has died by suicide. But ignoring emotions doesn't make them go away, and the only way to not be *forever sad* is to admit that we are, for the moment, *sad.*

Suicide isn't something people like to talk about, but that doesn't mean the feelings are going to disappear. They'll just come out in a different way, like tipping a bookshelf onto your sister or screaming at the top of your lungs until you lose your voice and you can't anymore. Death is private, but suicide belongs to everyone.

After the funeral, a flock of ladies descended upon our house. I still don't know who they were or how they knew us. I've never asked my dad, and for years if any woman looked at me for a second too long, I'd wonder if she had been one of them. They were all dressed up and they drank wine and I thought we were having a party. But it wasn't a party—it was a purging. They went through our house and stuffed everything that belonged to my mother in trash bags to be given away. These women were not just throwing my mother's things away—they were trying to throw *her* away, to erase her. When I realized what was occurring, I became a thief. I secretly grabbed all that my little hands could carry, which only amounted to her fur coat, a pair of Gucci shoes, and one photo album. We also had to give away our two adorable pugs, Mugsy and Sushi, because they had been my mom's dogs. My dad was working, and my brother and I were too young to be responsible for them. I wish I had been able to keep more of her clothes and other heirlooms, but I was denied this inheritance. I still wonder sometimes where my mom's clothes ended up and who in the world is wearing them.

The photo album I took dated back to my mother's teenage years and includes many pictures of her with young men who are most definitely *not* my dad. Some of the pictures had love notes written on the back. I would have liked to have more pictures of her with my family, but I also enjoyed daydreaming about what she was like in high school. I imagined what kind of teenager she was and if I would be like her when I was that age. She was pretty, and it seemed like lots of people liked her. Most of all, it seemed like she liked herself. I kept the photo album hidden in my closet along with her Gucci shoes, which seemed more like Christmas tree ornaments than shoes because her feet were so small. Her fur coat became my favorite article of clothing. I loved how it felt grand, worn, pre-loved.

Recently, I discovered that the photo album and the coat and the shoes aren't the only things I inherited from my mother. I learned on a podcast that all humans carry around a unique set of microbes that live on our skin, which "colonize" us as we pass through the birth canal. The microbes literally jump from our mother's uterus and vagina and set up shop on our newborn skin. Regardless of where we move around the world or the countless interactions we have throughout our life, our skin microbes will always be descendants from the original microbes we inherited from our mothers at birth.

I was devastated when I first learned this fact. Knowing that I literally carry my mother with me made me feel like I was infected with some dark thing. But then I came to feel comforted by this inheritance. What about those times in summer camp when everyone got sick but me? Or when boys tell me I smell nice even when I'm sweaty? It must have been her microbes. I look at how far I've come and I see that my mother's microbes have been my invisible teammates. I understand that even if her illness prevented her from raising me, part of her has been with me all along.

All dead people should know this: they're going to matter, even if they think they won't and even if they don't want to. I understand now that toward the end, my mother was so sick that she didn't want to be part of this world any longer. She thought she could fade away. But her absence meant as much to me as her presence would have. The older I get, the closer in age we get, since after all she will be that age forever. Peter Pan Mommy: I am catching up to her, and it will be weird when I am older than her.

Maybe my mom thought that she was being kind to

me by leaving—that because she was gone I wouldn't have to deal with having such a mother. That you're only real when you're alive. But by leaving the way she did, my mother actually burdened me with the task that would come to define my young adult life: to grow up without her.

Bravey Notes

- The imagination is an incredibly powerful tool that can comfort us, bring us joy, and even empower us to chase an impossible-seeming dream. Imagining things into existence is a superpower.

- You never know what you're going to remember; in fact, it's not even in your control. Sometimes it's the hard memories that stick with us most, and that's okay—pain takes its time.

if an oyster can turn sand into pearls
i can turn myself into anything.

GIRL SCOUTS

My brother taught me to pee standing up.
That's how people pee, duh. He'd also dress me up in
my dad's work suits and make me sit on the toilet with
a newspaper in my hands and wait for my dad to come
home. He would tell me, "See, this is how he does it." One
time my dad was late coming home and I waited for an
hour on the toilet reading an article I couldn't understand. My dad came home and found me, and that was
when he decided I needed to be around more women.

My dad has always liked traditional things. He or-
ders *classic* breakfasts like waffles, western omelets, and
eggs Benedict. He introduced me to *classic* sports like
baseball, soccer, basketball, and track. He still signs my
presents "From Santa." So naturally, when he sought out

female mentorship for me, he turned to the most classically female environment available: the Girl Scouts.

I was six years old when he first signed me up, and being at Girl Scout meetings felt like stepping through a kaleidoscope peephole into a glittery female world that both intimidated and fascinated me. Up until that point, I had only really been surrounded by men and animals: my dad, my brother, our pugs, and our cats. But my weekly Girl Scout meetings were the domain of *the mom*. The troop leaders were all moms and they'd lead us scouts in weekly meetings where we'd learn how to sew, do crafts, and cook pancakes on upside-down Folgers coffee tins with tea candles underneath. I felt more comfortable being the only girl at Boy Scouts than being surrounded by girls at Girl Scouts. (I know this because I went to multiple Boy Scout meetings and trips when it was my dad's turn to chaperone my brother's troop and he could not leave me home alone.) At Girl Scout meetings I felt the constant presence of a mom hovering over me in a way that was deeply unfamiliar. I had never felt a woman's chest accidentally brush against me before. Charm necklaces dangled onto my shoulder like fairies, and perfume cascaded over me as the mom-leaders helped stitch the crotch together on my pair of homemade pajamas. Other girls weren't distracted by the approach of a mom-leader and could keep working on their crafts despite being watched by mom-eyes, but not me. I was always transfixed when one of them turned her attention to me, and I couldn't focus on anything else. It felt like touching hot candle wax, where you want to do it and still keep doing it even though it hurts.

These moms were not like my mom at all. My mom, when she was home, was liable to explode into a fit of rage at any moment. She was not to be approached. I knew she would never harm me physically, but when she'd yell at the toaster in the kitchen because she thought it was talking to her, my instincts told me to keep my guard up.

At first I was wary and even afraid of these Girl Scout mom-leaders. It was overwhelming and strange to be around them, and I didn't like when they paid too much attention to me, as if to overcompensate for the things they thought I was missing at home; as if I didn't know exactly what I was missing, but *they did*. When the mom-leaders spoke to me, I fumbled in my interactions with them. I didn't know how to be disciplined by or properly receive a talking-to from a woman; I didn't know how to take a compliment or otherwise respond to *being mothered*. But I didn't want them to think I didn't know how. I tried to respond the way I felt you were supposed to because I wanted them to think I understood my role. I didn't want to be the poor little girl with the dead mom.

Within the incubator of my own home, I never felt *watched* like I did at Girl Scouts. In my recollection, nobody in my house watched me. My mom was the one who needed to be observed and helped. Most times when my mother and I were actually in the same space, which was rare, she seemed either to not realize I was there or to just not care. In the rare moments when my mom did look at me, she usually looked *through* me. And even though I *did* want a mom, a real mom, I also liked the freedom I had. I didn't like being watched so closely, so suddenly, so constantly. Sometimes attention feels good, but sometimes too much attention feels bad.

In a way, my mom and I were *both* allowed to be reckless around each other. She made me feel capable for reasons I still can't fully explain or justify. I don't mean to glorify her illness, I'm just saying that someone as tortured inside her own head as my mother was doesn't have the capacity to insert themselves into someone else's, for better and for worse. For better because when I was around her I had the unusual freedom to push the boundaries of my curiosity, and for worse because I knew if I asked her for help I wouldn't get it. My dad had his hands full balancing work with coming home on time for dinner, if he could—as long as my brother and I were physically safe, going to school, playing sports, and eating, the rest was up to us to figure out on our own.

* * *

My friends' parents, on the other hand, had attention to spare. I learned this from countless playdates at their houses, where their moms were not only present but *active participants,* enhancing the playdate with craft projects and snacks. I rarely had friends over because my dad worked so much, and even when he was home I never liked other people seeing the waist-high mountains of newspapers that covered the majority of our floor, or the general lack of rules and supervision at our house. My friends loved it because my house felt like a mystical playland, a break from the parental authority that typically governed their lives. To my friends, my house symbolized freedom. But to me, my friends' houses symbolized a thoughtfully supervised life that felt as enticing but untouchable as a picture on Instagram.

I do believe there's a healthy spectrum of parental attention that exists, with my dad closer to one end of the spectrum and a helicopter parent on the opposite end. But here's the thing: On the helicopter side of the spectrum, a parent's personal ego can become wrapped up in their kid's life. Maybe for a parent, the hardest thing to do is to let their kid fail. But I believe that reducing a child's pain to nothing is far worse.

There's a huge difference between opening doors for

your kid and pushing them through. My dad never told me to go to bed early, never wrote one of my essays for me, and never pointed out the pimples on my face. He didn't know my every movement, but he made sure I always had a safe way to get around and a safe place to stay. It was up to me to bounce within those barriers. I know that if I had felt even a drop of pressure from my dad, I might have burned out as a runner and never become an Olympian. It's not that my dad didn't care. Maybe he knew that, like my mom, I was always hardest on myself. It wouldn't have helped to be pushed. He never pushed. He bent over backward to ensure that I had opportunities—in middle school my dad would drive me from soccer practice to softball practice to cross-country meets, shielding me with a towel as I changed from one uniform into the next—but when we got to the activity, he let me do my thing.

For young Alexi, Girl Scouts was a weekly interruption to the life of independence I had at home with my dad and brother. I became self-conscious underneath the Scout moms' constant observation and I started questioning my every move. At the same time, I felt I was stronger and wiser than the other girls who had moms— how do you become confident and independent if you are constantly given a helping hand, even when you might not need it?

* * *

One time I peed in my sleeping bag during a Girl Scout camping trip, and I concocted an elaborate story about how a raccoon had entered the old manor where we all bunked, crept into my sleeping bag, and peed. I then went on to explain how I heroically scared it away before it could pee in anyone else's sleeping bag—thereby justifying the presence of urine in only my sleeping bag. All the girls believed me, but the mom-leaders pulled me aside and told me they knew I was lying, and lying was *very bad.* My dad had to make the hour-long drive to the campsite to deliver a fresh sleeping bag, but he didn't have anything to say about my raccoon cover story. This lie didn't actually hurt anybody. My dad knew when to let me take care of myself in the ways I knew how.

I know the Girl Scout moms made sure to notify him about my big lie, and I could tell that they were disappointed he didn't discipline me. This made me very angry. I've always hated it when I can tell that my dad feels judged by other parents, however subtly. There are lots of things most parents do that my dad never did.

But I knew that my dad loved me more than anything in the world, just in his own ways.

My dad had to leave the campsite shortly after making the sleeping-bag delivery because there were NO BOYS ALLOWED. I was sad to see him go—because, you see, this was that strange time in adolescence when I felt a distinct push and pull between genuinely wanting to spend time with my dad and also wanting him totally out of sight. I stewed in my shame, thinking I was destined to forever feel out of place in this Girl Scout world. But then the sun went down and the moms built a campfire and we sang songs and ate s'mores and I felt a shift, as if the darkness and the flickering campfire allowed me to blend in with the other girls and forget the thing that made me different. Being one silhouette among many gathered around the campfire felt deeply *good,* like the gooey center of a roasted marshmallow. It was the first time I can remember when I didn't feel responsible for myself. I was a part of a crowd of little girls and sillies, and I really appreciate that the moms let us kids *just be.* I finally allowed myself to fit in like one marshmallow among many.

I haven't officially quit the Girl Scouts. I think I may even still be a member on a list somewhere deep within my troop's archives. The troop moms will always hold a special place in my heart. I am sure I was as much a handful to them as they were to me. I want them to know it was worth the effort.

Bravey Notes

- Things that are helpful to some people might not be helpful to you. That's okay! Focus on what is useful for you.

- It's great to get help from your parents, but it's also important to learn how to be capable on your own, without their help.

i admire pickles because there is no one moment
that makes a pickle

a pickle. it is a thing that happens over time.
pickles are patient.

THE MENTOR BUFFET

I always appreciate when women I admire let me close to them. I never liked female mentorship when it was forced on me, as it was in Girl Scouts, but I *loved* it when I could seek it out on my own terms.

My first female mentors were the live-in au pairs my dad hired to stay with us during my elementary school days. They were always Eastern European women between nineteen and twenty-two years old and could only stay with us for one year at a time and not a day longer. This wasn't up to me, this was up to the government. My favorite au pair was Petra from the Czech Republic. Petra was calm but sharp. She never spoke to me like I was a little kid—she treated me like I was capable of speaking for myself, as if she were a high-end chef speaking to a distinguished diner: "And how is the macaroni and cheese tonight?" She asked what books I was reading and what they were about. She showed me how a woman can be confident and curious at the same time.

At home I followed Petra around, copying the things she ate and did and said. I attached myself to Petra like a well-intentioned leech. She wore plain white V-necked T-shirts that she made into tank tops, so I stole my dad's undershirts and cut the sleeves off to fashion them like hers. I felt much more capable when I imitated Petra than when I was being myself. I also copied Petra's basketball warm-up routine. She used to shoot hoops in our driveway every day, and I would spy on her from the window. I'm fairly certain she could see my little face smashed against the glass, but she never said anything. I appreciated that she let me watch her without pointing it out. It can be embarrassing to admire someone so much, and I needed to be able to copy her without her acknowledging that I was copying her. By letting my observations and imitations pass unspoken, Petra helped me grow the invisible muscle called *confidence* while also preserving my dignity.

After the era of au pairs ended, my infusions of female mentorship came from my best friends' moms. Until the day I left for college I had a lineup of moms inviting me

over for dinner or bringing me to nail salons or chaperon-
ing me at concerts. I had a special relationship with these
moms—if a friend and her mom were arguing about how
we weren't allowed to leave the house to walk around our
small city after dark, the mom would always turn to me,
as if performing an aside in a play, and smile, shrug her
shoulders, and say, "That's just how it is! I know, I know,
I'm a mean mom."

As a non-mommed kid, I could never be fully folded
into the mother-daughter dynamic. I existed somewhere
outside of that. I was not a daughter with a mother of her
own waiting at home (moms seem to generally know not
to encroach on each other's territory) nor was I an adult
peer. I was an exciting project. This was a role I was glad
to fill—because it came with benefits. I was allowed to be
present with friends and their moms in moments when
an outsider might not normally be included, like going to
the pool and not being asked to leave the bathroom stall
when it was the mom's turn to change. This is how I was
introduced to the adult vagina. I remember all the mom-
vaginas I ever saw because it felt like seeing a sea otter in
San Francisco Bay: not impossible but definitely not an
everyday occurrence. It was fascinating to catch a glimpse
of what I might expect from my own body one day. I am
very grateful for the moms who did this for me without

even realizing it. I also absorbed tremendous amounts of knowledge and wisdom from women I didn't know at all, whom I'd observe in brief moments throughout my everyday life: at the grocery store, or in a dentist's waiting room, or in a public restroom while the lady next to me examined her face in the mirror. I was a highly adept observer, logging every small detail in just a few seconds. With each new tidbit of womanly knowledge I gleaned, the world of the feminine widened a bit. In middle school my friend Kati's mom often invited me over for dinner after school because she knew my dad worked late, and by then I was too old for au pairs but too young to be responsible for meals every night after school, practice, and homework. I probably ate dinner with Kati's family twice a week. Two family dinners per week is an above-average amount to be eating at your friend's house, but it was either go to Kati's, where there was a thoughtfully prepared meal, or be at home alone. My dad often worked well past the dinner hour and I'd be left to cook for myself. I knew he was doing the best he could, and he cooked great meals when he was able, but I have always loved good food and I've never been too proud to seek it out. Food is more than just calories, it's also love. Food is a love battery.

I think Kati's mom invited me over not just for my own well-being but also because I genuinely loved the food she fed me and wasn't shy about expressing my gratitude. With each dish she placed before me, my excitement and awe were palpable. I would ask her, "What *is* this? How did you make this?" Every week she prepared things I'd never heard of before—panzanella, paella, and other dishes that perhaps were ordinary to her but that I thought were magnificent. She was always more than willing to take the time to answer my questions, like how often she went grocery shopping and how long to boil oatmeal and whether butter should be kept in the fridge or not. I learned that having genuine curiosity and gratitude was the best way to start a conversation with someone I hoped to learn something from.

I'd always ask Kati if we could do our homework at the kitchen table instead of upstairs in her bedroom. The view and the smells in the kitchen were wonderfully distracting, and I think Kati's mom knew I was watching her. I felt reassured by her presence. I pretended she was cooking especially for me as she layered lasagna, and this made me feel loved in a way that I craved as much as I craved that lasagna. I imagined she laid the pasta sheets down atop the tomato sauce in the same way that she tucked her kids into bed at night. Why focus on algebra, which has been around forever and isn't going anywhere, when you can absorb something much more fleeting and rare, like the sight of a mom making your dinner? I was prepped from very early in life to understand that some things last and some things do not. I always got seconds and thirds at Kati's house and I even took home leftovers. All I wanted to do was absorb more of that lasagna and more of that mom.

I asked Kati's mom to help me understand how I could become a good cook. Kati didn't need this knowledge yet, but I needed it now, since I was cooking dinner for myself a couple of times a week. I needed to understand how to love myself like Kati's mom loved her family. Food is a good way to show love to yourself. The meal I am most proud of was from a recipe Kati's mom shared with me. It is a beef pot roast that cooks itself during the day while you're not even home to watch it. I was so proud the first time I made that pot roast and arrived home to find my perfect treasure in the oven after a full day of anticipation. As I ate, I decided that I *liked* asking moms for advice and that I'd do it more often. In high school, I asked Kati's mom to help me sew my sophomore Winter Ball dress out of found fabric. She said yes without hesitation. I realize that the stories in this chapter revolve around food, sewing, and beauty—but it was never the actual act of baking a cake or cooking a meal or sewing a dress that affected me, it was the *confidence* that Kati's mom and other women like her brought to their actions, confidence that was so strong and deep that I couldn't help but absorb some of it myself.

It didn't feel dumb to ask for help from people I admired, and in fact, I learned that it felt better to ask for help than to wait until someone noticed I needed it. Mentorship is a two-way street. It's not passive, it's active, and you can ask for it. Asking for help is a superpower anyone can have but only some people use. It is brave to ask for help. Asking for help is the first step toward finding a mentor. Mentors can help us change our lives if we let them.

* * *

A good mentor is a living example of the type of person you'd like to be, and you can learn from them simply by being in their vicinity and paying attention. And the older I got, the more my hunger for mentors grew. I was always on the lookout. The summer after college, I spent several weeks in Provincetown, Massachusetts, with my friend Abbey's aunt Mary and Mary's partner, Marion. Marion and Auntie Mary were in their sixties and had the vibrancy of teenagers. I felt lucky to be allowed into their space and I was happy to make their routines my own. I sat at their kitchen table like a kid after school, eating blueberries and listening to them talk. They wanted to hear about my silly little movie, *Tracktown,* which at the time was just an idea. But the way they asked me about it made it seem like it *could* be real, like my idea wasn't silly and I should take myself seriously. They never told me this directly—they didn't have to. I am forever grateful to them and the gift they gave me by simply being themselves and letting me be around them. Their confidence gradually stuck to me, like I was walking through their perfume every day until it became part of my own aura.

I learned that I thrive when I'm around people who believe in themselves and in me. When I began life as an Olympic hopeful, I often took extended training trips to Mammoth Lakes, California, just to be closer to my biggest athletic role model, Deena Kastor, an Olympic bronze medalist and the American record holder for the marathon. I had always admired Deena from afar, but when she invited me to visit and train with the Mammoth Track Club, their training group, I leapt at the opportunity. When someone you admire that much gives you the chance to get close to them, you take it. I got nervous for every single long run and workout that I did with Deena, and there was one particular two-hour run that felt especially daunting. It was the longest run I'd ever done, and a long run is a hard thing to fake. The distance and pace were ambitious, but I didn't want to drop out early; I wanted to be alongside Deena for as long as possible. Sure enough, about an hour and a half into the run, I sensed the hurt coming on. The trail felt like hummus under my feet. My legs felt like two cylinders of canned cranberry sauce, splatting just a bit more with each step. If I had been alone, I would have slowed down. But that wasn't an option here. So I shifted my attention away from my own pain and instead focused on Deena. Specifically, I focused on her breath, which was calm compared to mine. I pretended she was breathing for both of us. In moments like this, an individual sport like running becomes a team sport. Deena sensed my pain and distracted me by pointing out a passing hawk and trying to guess where it came from and where it was heading. I held on to our pace for the sake of hearing the rest of Deena's hawk fable. No one had told me spontaneous stories like this when I was a child, and I relished it deep in the youngest place in my heart.

Deena made me feel like a more capable athlete and she also made me feel like a more capable person. She pushed me from a place of magnanimous love. To be pushed by someone who truly believes in you is a huge gift. It is like they're pushing you and pulling you at the same time. It is a love that comes from a place of wanting you to be there with them.

Knowing I may never be in the same room as the people I look up to has never stopped me from making them into mentors. I've learned how to look up to women I admire from afar, which takes the same kind of imagination my little-girl self used when I pretended someone else's mom was mine. For instance, even though I've never met the famous cooking show host Melissa Clark, I feel like I've drawn as much comfort from watching her *New York Times* food videos as I did from watching Kati's mom cook. When I watch Melissa's videos I pretend she is my mom telling me how to make a crumble—joking that it doesn't really matter if the strawberries are chopped perfectly because people don't like perfect! If you're feeling brave, add mint! She taught me that it is better to be brave, not perfect. With Melissa, I always try to listen to what she's actually saying beneath the recipe itself. What she means when she says she is going to save the crisp edges of the casserole for herself is that she values herself enough to give herself the best part of her creation. She is kind to herself first.

Britney Spears is another example: she taught me to unapologetically commit to my goals after I read in a magazine that as a child she used to take over the family bathroom to sing into her hairbrush because she knew she was destined to be a singer when she grew up. She took her dreams seriously, and I latched on to that idea like a barnacle.

When I was little other people believed that I lacked something because of my mother's death. I can never know for sure exactly what I missed out on. But what I do know is that her death forced me to seek out female mentorship on my own terms, and the mother-shaped hole in my heart has now been filled by wonderful women of my choosing. My greatest loss has become my greatest gift: I've learned that the whole world and all its inhabitants are there for me to observe, absorb, and imitate. I will never outgrow or be too proud for mentors. I will always see the value in asking questions. Even though my mother's experiences are forever closed to me, the rest of the world is wide open.

Bravey Notes

- Asking for help isn't a weakness—it's actually a strength.

- Approaching someone you admire and asking for advice is inviting them to become a mentor. Not everyone accepts the invitation, but it's okay to ask. Mentorship is a two-way street: sometimes it's offered to you, but you can also seek it out.

- A good mentor is an example of the type of person you'd like to be. You can even have a mentor who you've never met—people you read about who are inspiring.

before bed, decide tomorrow will be great.

PUBERTY POWER

It was 2015 and my family and I stood together in the small waiting room just outside the Oval Office of the White House, nervously smiling like a group of kids waiting their turn at the top of a waterslide. My brother, Louis, stood at the front of our pack, ready to walk in first—he had spent the past few years working on President Obama's staff and this was his last day on the job. As such, he was invited to bring his family for a meet-and-greet with Obama himself. The Oval Office door cracked open and laughter spilled out into the waiting room. The family ahead of us walked out, and there he was: the president of the United States, standing just a few feet away.

One by one, we shook President Obama's hand. Louis introduced me as a professional runner. President Obama's attention turned to me. "You have a gift," he said. "You were born with a body that was meant to run long distances, more than the average human."

Right away I knew what I wanted to say in response . . . but did I dare risk embarrassing my brother by disagreeing with President Obama, his former boss and the most powerful person in the country? I started by thanking the president, and then I couldn't help myself—I added that my performance in the sport was just a result of hard work, motivation, and support from my community. But the president disagreed.

"No, no," he said. "Your body is able to flush out lactic acid better than the average person—running is what you were born to do." Obama's energy and tone was so confident and convincing that he could have told me the moon is really made out of cheese and I would have agreed with him. I nodded and thanked him. Besides, our five-minute meeting time was up. I left the Oval Office feeling very honored, but I also couldn't stop thinking about what the president had said. The idea that I was meant to run, that I was born with a special ability, felt like it subtracted from my own willpower and motivation.

My brother later told me that President Obama was a serious basketball player as a teenager and competed on one of the best high school teams in the country. He grew up training tirelessly, presumably with big basketball dreams, and it wasn't until later that he hung up his jersey and focused his attention elsewhere—though basketball was still near and dear to his heart. The thing was, as Obama grew up, he discovered that there were physical barriers that prevented him from advancing to compete at the highest level of basketball. No matter how hard he worked, he wasn't as tall or fast or coordinated as his competitors. That must have been deeply frustrating and heartbreaking to someone as driven and disciplined as President Obama.

* * *

In middle school and early high school, it's safe to say that natural ability was a huge factor in my athletic prowess. With a wiry body and unusually long limbs, I managed to become one of the top young runners in California. I finished fourth in the state my sophomore year. At the same time, I was also developing an interest in other things—student government, theater, competitive soccer, and a social life. I was preoccupied with what it would be like to grow up, where to go to college, what I wanted to be, dreaming of change (all types of it), new foods, new friends. I dreamt of all the good things and all the bad things that could happen, I dreamt of my face on a magazine with big headlines of creating something new, I feared the bad people in our world, I feared I would get sucked into an apocalypse of sadness and never get out. My ambitions and my fears were well-rounded.

But being a well-rounded teenager was not what my high school's athletic leadership wanted. At the beginning of junior year, my track coach, along with the head of my high school's athletic department, gave me an ultimatum: I would need to quit soccer or I would be kicked off the track team. He felt it was right and best to force high school athletes to specialize. The system itself was structured to benefit athletes who specialized and punish those with a diversity of commitments. Not all athletes, to be clear— only female athletes. There were multi-sport male athletes at our school who were celebrated, but for some reason the women's running coach (who was a man) felt that we needed to erase the other parts of our identities to succeed, as if a fifteen-year-old girl who had to miss a few practices represented a threat to the athletic department's author-ity. They wanted me to be a compliant good girl. I wasn't a bad girl, but I wanted to be treated respectfully. There was not a single woman in this whole conversation—the entire school leadership was men. My father and I made an official complaint to the school leadership but we were disregarded. My dad even consulted with a lawyer, but ul-timately decided not to pursue the case because private Catholic schools have minimal accountability beyond their own internal decision making. This was the most potent encounter with sexism I've ever had in my life—being unabashedly told that I was being held to a different standard than the boys within the high school athletic system.

Since I didn't want to quit soccer, I was not allowed to be on the cross-country or track teams and I didn't run that year. Then, in my senior year, I tried to re-join the cross-country team. The coach once again made it clear that he would not permit anyone to miss or reschedule anything, especially if the conflict was with any other extracurricular activities. This came to a head for me during Spirit Week, which is a very big deal at Bishop O'Dowd High School. It is the biggest week of the year, full of themed days and bonding activities. During Spirit Week each grade was responsible for decorating a section of hallway in a particular theme. And when I say "decorate," I mean it was tradition to *cover* your entire section with a full 3-D set. We were the "Super Nintendo Seniors." We had worked for weeks on the hallway decorations and, as the class vice president, I was personally responsible for ensuring that the decorations went up in time. I asked my coach to let me miss practice for a day so that I could be there during the final pre–Spirit Week decorating push, but he said no, I had to be at practice, and if I wasn't there then I'd be kicked off the team. I missed practice and that was that—the end of my high school running career.

I wish the coach had seen that as a high schooler, I did not feel ready to specialize in anything, especially a sport that I was good at but had not yet fallen in love with. I was slowly learning to enjoy running, but it was not for the reasons he was trying to force on me. I was a late bloomer; I always have been. And I was gradually growing into the sport just as I was gradually growing into myself. The things I liked about running were the moments when sport felt *fun*. We were one of the best teams in the state. But we were also teenagers. The minute the coach set unreasonable boundaries for us, it stopped being fun and started feeling too serious. All the joy was gone—and I strongly believe that joy is not mutually exclusive to performance.

That's what I like about all sports that I've ever played, when they bring me joy. I've always looked for joy and fun first in sports, and the environment around the sport is as much a factor as the sport itself. When I was little, I tried gymnastics—which I think I could have found fun—but the instructors at my particular gym were very harsh and strict, they would press down on my back with their feet to force me to do splits, and it did not feel fun. The gym was built in a converted movie theater, and I'd sneak away in the middle of class to explore empty rooms and play with abandoned film equipment. So I suppose I have gymnastics to thank for my movie career.

The point is, the focus of high school sports should be on human development, not high achievement. Competition results are a byproduct, not the end goal. I'm glad my dad never pushed me to specialize in running at a young age—he and I both knew I was good, but my dad's top priority was seeing me thrive as a person. He'd rather me be a happy normal kid than a stressed-out running star. I wanted to experience things. I was in the school play, I partied, I experimented. I was curious. Nothing too extreme, but probably not the type of behavior most parents would associate with a future Olympian. If you look at a snapshot of me in any one moment of my high school life, you probably wouldn't guess where I would end up. I settled comfortably into puberty, allowing my body to morph into whatever proportions it needed as I grew and changed. There were several months where I grew bigger boobs than I've ever had, and a distinctly round belly, which my best friends lovingly named *Tommy the Tummy*, not to shame me, but to adore my ever-changing body and celebrate it. In turn, I had no problem with it and celebrated it. Look, I know that it isn't healthy to have a potbelly, but I also know that I was generally being healthy and normal, and my body—for whatever reason—took on a certain shape as it developed. Fighting against that natural development would have sabotaged my development, my happiness, and my future.

I also understand that it is not easy to feel comfortable in a changing body. Not everyone would find "Tommy" very funny, and I feel lucky that I had a great group of friends, a dad who wasn't examining me too closely, and also that I grew up before social media. I was in my own little bubble of acceptance. To not feel at home in your own body is the hardest feeling, because your body follows you everywhere. Everywhere you go, there you are. So much of our identity can be tied up in our body—and for athletes especially, feeling like you're fighting a losing battle against your own body can feel frustrating. One trick to cope is to find a new activity to try as your body changes. I mentor a girl who could not run the way she was used to during puberty. So she tried boxing. It was strange at first, to punch a bag instead of sprinting up a hill every day. But she loved the way boxing made her feel; she felt powerful. She still ran, just less. For me, I played more soccer during those years when I didn't run. As a center defender, my developing body was a welcomed addition to the team. I thrived because I was in an environment where I liked what my body could do. I still wanted to run and trusted that I could run at a high level again in time, but for the moment, it was healthy to change my activities to match where my body was at that moment. Not just match, thrive! We all want to feel capable, and that sometimes comes down to the environment we put ourselves in. When a goldfish grows, you need to change the bowl.

The ironic twist is that my forced retirement from high school running became a major advantage in my later growth as an NCAA and then professional athlete. I inadvertently stopped training just long enough for my body to go through puberty without the strain of over-training, which is exactly the challenge that most girls in distance running face at that age.

The vast majority of athletic programs, even at the collegiate level, lack the most fundamental information about how to properly guide female athletes through puberty and young adulthood. Programs confuse *health* with *fitness.* Fitness is not an indicator of durability and sustainability; it is only an indicator of athletic ability at the present moment. Health, on the other hand, is a more holistic measure of the body's functionality over time. Fitness does not take into account that you need to continue training tomorrow and next week. It is better to be a hundred percent healthy and eighty percent fit than a hundred percent fit and eighty percent healthy. It's like good pasta: best to be slightly undercooked.

But that's not the way most programs see things. Fitness is rewarded while health is taken for granted. I don't think this approach always comes from a bad place, it just comes from ignorance—and the unfortunate result is that when female athletes hit puberty, they'll often take short-cuts to fitness at the expense of their long-term health. When a girl's body transitions from adolescence into adulthood, the physical changes that occur can seem—at first—to be counterproductive to fitness, mainly weight gain as her frame expands and her body fills out. I once consoled a college teammate after the coach called her into his office and made her hold a five-pound weight in each hand and pump her arms as if she was running, and then had her put the weights down and pump her arms again—a demonstration of how much easier it is to run after losing ten pounds. So in an effort to please their coaches and keep up with their male teammates, whose developmental trajectory is completely different, many female athletes overtrain and don't eat enough during this critical growth phase instead of allowing puberty to naturally take its course. (I know female athletes whose periods were delayed until their twenties.)

The result of this systemic prioritization of fitness over health for young female athletes is that many girls will become frail and injury-prone by the time they're in college—as a result of eating disorders. As I grew up and became captain of various sports teams, it was always hard for me to see someone relating to the sport, to their body, or to anyone else in a way that felt unhealthy. It was easy for me to be angry with them. This happens all the time. We get mad at our teammates and friends when we see them in harmful situations. But really the anger is not for them. The anger is for the system that puts our teammates in situations where their health is at odds with their fitness. I am angry at the system, not at the person.

The anger also comes with a side of sadness. It breaks my heart to think of all the young women who quit the sport because the system made them feel as if they "weren't built for distance running." To me, that is the biggest tragedy, when somebody gives up on a dream because of being mishandled or otherwise rushed due to a system that does not work. When the same bad things happen to a group of people time and time again, it is important to look closer at the failed system that is responsible. We are failing ourselves if we don't.

* * *

After I stopped running my junior year, my coaches assumed that I'd be lost to the vortex of puberty that claims so many female runners. But what none of them knew is that rather than being a death sentence, puberty is a superpower. The body that I grew during my junior and senior years of high school was capable, durable, and powerful because I wasn't fighting against my body's natural inclinations. I grew C-cup boobs. I rode the puberty wave and then, when the time was right, I gradually increased my training. My mature body was far more durable and powerful and capable than the twisted Peter Pan prepubescent body that most female athletes feel pressured to maintain. It is a problem to assume that if we allow a girl to go through normal body maturity, she will never again be as capable as she was pre-puberty. It's straight-up wrong, because in reality, most female distance runners peak in their late twenties and early thirties. Our bodies take time to develop. Why can't *develop* be a word we embrace?

Starting as early as middle and high school, we can educate coaches and athletes on the proper approach that young women can take to embrace their bodies and stay healthy and ultimately grow into more capable adults. I hope that one day it can become common knowledge that female bodies operate on different performance timelines than their male teammates and require a different type of support.

* * *

When I started college, it was expected that I would join the cross-country team. Dartmouth's recruiters had reached out to me on the basis of my performance my sophomore year of high school, and the coach was interested in my potential. I also saw a future for myself in running and I liked the idea of committing to a sport where I could chase big dreams. I was curious. And unlike the coaches who wanted me to specialize in high school, in college I found a coach and team who inspired me instead of pressured me. I felt ready and even happy to embrace running. But when I reported to my first practice, it became abundantly clear that I would no longer breeze to the top of the ranks as I had in middle school and early high school. I couldn't rely on my talent alone. After two years away from competitive running, my body had changed. It was humiliating to have to walk after only a few miles on easy training runs while my teammates literally ran circles on the trails around me. I finished dead last in my first cross-country race. I was not only the last on my team; I had one of the slowest times in the whole league. Running wasn't the only part of college life I struggled with: My adjustment to Dartmouth's academics felt like falling into an ice-cold lake—it was a shock, and I could barely keep my head above water. One of my professors called me in for a special meeting after I failed yet another multiple-choice midterm and asked if I might have a learning disability. Anytime I failed a test, I had a sad little tradition where I'd take myself out to Ramunto's, a pizza spot in Hanover, and treat myself to several garlic-knot pizza slices, where the crust is actually made of garlic knots. I ate at Ramunto's more often than I'd like to admit.

I knew that, like my fitness, my grades wouldn't magically improve on their own. It was going to take hard work. I visited my professors outside of class nearly every day to review the questions I got wrong on a test or how I could improve an essay. And slowly, over time, I learned how to be an Ivy League student. I learned how to focus during long lectures and how to write an analytical essay. I feel grateful that I had the intellectual capacity to teach myself these things, but I certainly would have failed out of Dartmouth without an incredible amount of hard work. The same principle held true with my running: My athletic talent was there, but it needed to be molded by hard work. It was going to be painful and humbling and slow, but I agreed with myself to keep showing up and not give up on myself, no matter how hard it got. The good news and the bad news about not giving up is that it works. It's good because you *can* achieve what you set your mind to; it's bad (or at least unpleasant) because, well, it won't be easy.

Those first few semesters in college were a long trudge toward getting my fitness back. In time, six-mile runs became ten-mile runs, and six hours of sleep became nine.

I stopped failing tests, so garlic-knot pizzas phased out of my regular routine. I also learned more about nutrition. In my dad's house, food was just food. He never used words like *healthy* or *unhealthy,* just like he never used words like *pretty* or *ugly,* which I appreciate deeply. I didn't have harmful complexes about food, for which I am very grateful, but I also didn't have basic knowledge of how to fuel properly.

Food can be a sensitive subject for female distance runners, harkening back to the pressure that most girls face to stay thin even as their bodies are desperately trying to develop and mature. But longevity and durability should be part of the conversation as well. And it *should* be a conversation; we should not be silent about food. At Dartmouth, some girls on my team made a practice of limiting their portions by only eating from the palm-sized side-dish bowls in our cafeteria, never actual plates. When I became captain, I instituted a rule that you had to eat proper portions off a real plate.

In the meantime, while I was not fit enough to contribute to the team in a competitive sense, I contributed in other ways. When the traveling squad went to New York City for the Ivy League Cross Country Championships, I found my own transportation to the race and went in costume to cheer them on. My costume was a full snakeskin bodysuit and I cheered at the top of a big hill alongside a boy from Brown dressed as the Burger King, mask and all. In this way, even when I was not fit enough to score a team point, I could still find ways to matter by staying engaged, leaning in, and contributing any way I knew how. It built my self-worth and gave me a purpose every day while my body caught up. It takes integrity, determination, humility, and, most of all, a sense of humor to be the team mascot when just a few years earlier I would have easily beaten any of these girls. I kept showing up and I'm proud of how I handled myself during those few years. Yes, *years*. It wasn't until the winter of my junior year that I contributed my first team point.

In my senior year, I competed in an NCAA Track and Field Championship for the first time. By then, the prepubescent Alexi who placed high in state championship meets as a tween was long gone. The new Alexi was made from endless work, discipline, patience, and good pain (and lots of sleep). Stepping up to the start line for the first leg of the distance medley relay at the NCAA Indoor Championships felt like something I had fought for and earned. I even got matching tattoos with my relay teammates because we were so proud. We had set a lofty goal, worked hard, and made it happen.

I am grateful that I had the opportunity to safely and naturally grow a body durable enough to withstand the level of effort it took to make it all the way to the Olympics. I'm also grateful that I had the natural talent somewhere inside me to develop into a world-class runner, as President Obama said. I appreciate that someone else might have worked just as hard as me without achieving the same results. But if talent gave me a powerful engine, then hard work (and plenty of good food) was my fuel. An engine is useless without the fuel.

I don't know if being a good athlete comes down to being born gifted or working hard. We can't know; it is always some combination of the two. I would also say that a third factor, *health*, is an equally important ingredient for athletic success. I hope that in the future, new generations of female runners will come of age in an environment that sets them up for long-term durability. Because no matter how powerful the engine and how potent the fuel, the whole thing is useless if it burns out too soon.

The biggest takeaway is this: We can't control the engine we're given. But how we treat our engine is entirely up to us. It will take us to the moon if we let it.

Bravey Notes

- It's better to be 100 percent healthy and 80 percent fit than the other way around.

- Sometimes puberty can make you feel awkward in your own body, but embracing puberty as a strength allows you to become a more mature, durable, and capable version of yourself.

- Talent is one factor in determining future success, but it's not the *only* factor. Hard work and health are just as important.

chasing a dream is like building a sandcastle.

every grain of sand is important, even
if you can't see them all.

CRUSH

The first crush I ever had was on an animated dog named Max from a movie called *A Goofy Movie*, which came out in 1995, three months after my mom died. Max was a semi-rebellious skater dog-teenager who I found charming and hot. My best friend, Amanda, first showed me the movie, the two of us sitting on her couch sipping chocolate milk. I remember watching the movie like I normally watched cartoons, mostly following the plot and maybe seeing myself in one of the characters, absorbing and laughing, when all of a sudden I was hit with a distinct sensation. I felt a little flutter in my heart, like a butterfly was flapping its wings. It was ticklish but on the inside. It felt good to feel things. My friend and the room and the entire world disappeared into a blur around me, and I became obsessed. I was fixated on Max.

My imagination leapt to think about what it might be like to kiss this . . . cartoon dog? I daydreamed that I was a dog, too, so Max and I could skate around the city of Spoonerville together. I imagined us doing things that would never happen because Max did not even know my name, because Max was also not real. I felt comfortable having a crush on an animated dog. It made me feel wild and excited but also very much *in control,* because I knew what was going to happen: nothing. He would never love me back, but he would also never reject me. He had no power over me. He existed entirely *for* me.

Right away, in the very first moments of my very first crush, I was already wrestling with the fear of rejection. You're vulnerable when you have a crush, because as soon as you admit that you like someone, you're opening yourself up to the possibility that they won't like you back. It almost doesn't seem fair that the wondrous feeling of *crushing* always goes hand in hand with the weight of possible rejection.

Still, I crushed hard, because love was something I wanted fiercely. I had only seen romance in movies, never in real life. I did not grow up seeing affection. My mom was certainly not affectionate, and my dad has never been outwardly affectionate. Sentimental, yes; loving, yes; affectionate, no. My only memory of my parents relating to each other was as caretaker to sick person, never as two grown-ups in romantic love. My family said "I love you" at home, but when my dad said "I love you," it was with the tone of needing to be heard, as if I might die and need to know this information, like how you need to know how to tie a certain kind of knot to survive in the wild. It was not delivered with the spontaneity of someone experiencing the feeling bursting through their heart straight into your chest. I wanted that feeling more than anything, and not even the fear that my crush might not like me back could stop me.

My first crush on a real-life human happened on a waterslide when I was eight years old. It was 1998 and it was the best year of my life so far. My dad took my brother and me on a very special vacation to a resort in Hawaii, and I was allowed to go on the waterslides alone (one of the first times I was allowed to sort of be alone). The line for the waterslides in August was as long as the beachfront, and I stood in line behind a boy who was also alone. My memory of him is an abstract painting—I can't remember any details. I remember nothing except the sudden punch in my gut that told me I adored and wanted to kiss this person. I had never considered what my dream crush would look like, but here he was. It surprised me, like when you unexpectedly hear a song on the radio that you love and it sounds even better than if you actually decided to play that song. It's the surprise-and-delight factor. A crush is a goal that can smile back at you.

I cherished our short ten-minute wait together—I nervously adjusted my butterfly hairclips; ubiquitous for girls in the '90s and a sure sign that I was not ahead of my time, I was very much *of* my time—and then watched him leap down the slippery incline and slide away from me. I went down the slide after waiting the obligatory ten seconds prescribed for safety and followed in his wake. I rocketed out of the slide and plunged into the water, then burst above the surface like a majestic dolphin, fully expecting to find my crush waiting for me. But when I opened my eyes, he wasn't there. You know the moment right after you've been completely submerged underwater and the burst of air and sunlight feels disorienting? That was how this felt, but to my heart. My crush was gone. I looked everywhere, but he was nowhere to be found. What did I expect? That he would be waiting there to catch me? No. I was alone, standing totally still in a mess of colors and chlorine and light. I thought I would see him somewhere by the poolside tiki bar, but it didn't happen. I never saw him again. I thought about him for the rest of the trip. But what did I think about, really? I liked the *idea* of him more than I actually liked him, because of course, I didn't *know* him. But crushes don't have to be known. They just want to be felt. And when you feel them, you feel them hard. I was heartbroken. It was the *lost potential* that got to me most. What if he was the love of my life, but now we could never be together because we never had the chance?

Before there is love, there is potential. The potential might last only moments before it blossoms into love, as it did for my grandparents—my yiayia fell in love at first sight with my papou and married him ten days later—or it might take years. Love unfolds differently for everyone, but it always begins as potential. If you think your crush might have the potential to be someone you could love, that is the moment when you have to decide how to view that person: with skepticism or with optimism, with arms folded or with arms open. It's safer to be skeptical; you're less likely to get hurt. Optimism takes courage. It's like chasing a dream. You need to give it a chance, because love, like a dream, is not something that the world hands to you. You have to be brave to believe in potential.

* * *

There are phases to having a crush. The first phase is curiosity. In this very early phase, my crush is like a seed in the ground: it's pure potential but nothing real, not yet. And by being curious, by thinking and imagining what this feeling I have might be, I am watering the seed. Sometimes my curiosity runs dry and the seed never sprouts. But most often (I am a person who crushes easily), the crush-seed takes root in my mind and begins to grow.

I tread lightly at first: after I realize I'm crushing on someone, I keep my distance. The person is blissfully unaware that they are on my radar, and I am also blissfully unaware because I have no indication of whether they might like me back. I haven't put any feelers out or otherwise suggested to the person that I like them. In this phase, my imagination runs wild—the other person is like a blank canvas. Because I don't know how the person really feels, they are whatever I imagine them to be. Every cell inside my body is lifted by tiny hot-air balloons, causing me to hover just above earth, suspended in a bubble of my own daydreams. My crush is constantly in my mind somewhere, sometimes at the forefront, sometimes nestled in the back, but definitely always there. It's like having someone with me all the time. It feels like they're there even when they're not. I wonder how this person became so important to me. I always want more, not less.

When I am with the person, I have trouble making eye contact with them. When I do make eye contact with them, I have trouble looking away. I hold my gaze a bit too long. I feel clumsy. What I mean is that I overthink everything and also can't think at all. I become obsessed with the littlest things about them: their eyes, their fingers, their skin. They can do nothing wrong. I assume I think about them more than they think about me. Social media adds another dimension to crushing, because it gives us a place to perform for one person while masked in a public performance: you may be posting *to* everyone, but you're really just posting *for* one person. It's like turning in a math problem without showing your work. With math problems, you want to show all your work. With crushes and dating, you want your proof of work to vanish. You don't want people to know your process, only how you make them feel at the end.

The second phase of a crush happens when I cross the line from the imaginary world into the real world and tell my crush how I feel. Now, it's worth noting that not every crush actually makes it to this second phase. In fact, most crushes don't. But there are some crushes that are like an itch I can't stop scratching, and I need to *do something* about it or else I'll explode. It's as scary as it is exciting, because I generally consider myself to be a rational and reasonable and calculating person, none of which are compatible with having a raging crush.

I never know quite how to talk to a crush. I'm always afraid I'll use words that would freak the other person out or come across as overly aggressive or "too much." I'm afraid I won't be able to fully identify the feelings I'm having. Or if I know what the feelings are, I'm afraid I'll pick the wrong words to represent them. I am afraid I will be rejected by the person because of the things I might say. I am afraid I will be misunderstood, one of the worst feelings in the world. I want another person and I want them to want what I want. I want them to like me back and I want them to be the way I imagine them to be and I want them to be as obsessed with me as I am with them. There is this crazy buildup of anticipation: I'm holding this crush without anyone knowing. I feel too afraid or embarrassed to admit it to the crush, and admitting it—saying it out loud, even to a friend—is like stepping off a cliff or starting a roller coaster. You are putting something in motion and it's going to be scary, and you don't know how it will end. It's uncomfortable, but it's also wonderful. But it doesn't always feel wonderful. Because what if it turns out badly?

The third and final phase of a crush is when my feelings have finally been spoken out loud and the crush either blossoms into a relationship or, if the other person doesn't feel the same as me, withers away into nothingness. The hardest part of this phase is that I have no control over what will happen. I've expressed myself as best I can and now it's in my crush's hands, because I cannot control how another person feels.

I used to feel devastated when a crush went unreciprocated. It felt like something was wrong with me. If you have your heart broken, the two things you will likely feel are rejection (and all the symptoms of that) and loneliness. Is it sad or not sad to be rejected? It's sad because you wanted to be liked back. But on the other hand, it's not sad, because the truth is this person was never yours to begin with, or is no longer yours, in the case of a breakup. Some crushes are like unripe fruit—they just weren't ready for you yet. Honesty doesn't always feel good in the moment, but it can cause the kind of pain that forces you forward.

As far as loneliness goes, that's a real thing. And the opposite of loneliness is being seen. You can be seen by things besides the one person you'd like to see you the most. You can feel seen by a song that feels like you feel; you can feel seen by a friend if you're willing to share with them; you can even be seen by someone preparing you a comforting meal. Most importantly . . . you might feel angry, but underneath it, you need to be seen by yourself. Just like you recognized that you had a crush or were in love, you also recognize the pain and the melancholy of letting go. And when you really think about it, it is so brave to watch yourself admit the loss and grow up right in front of yourself. Effort and vulnerability is beautiful.

Here is the truth: we can't control other people. We can only listen to our feelings and deliver them to others with the best intentions, like when you plant a seed and hope it will grow. There are so many other factors to how the plant will turn out that are beyond your control. If it was meant to be, it will be. If it wasn't, it won't. What's meant for you will stay with you. Yes, rejection hurts. But what hurts more than being rejected by someone else is rejecting yourself. Rejecting your own feelings because you're afraid that you might get hurt is the cruelest thing in the world.

The act of accepting your own feelings is an act of seeing yourself, presumably the very thing you want from your crush anyway. Being seen makes you feel loved. And seeing yourself is one way to love yourself. Loving yourself is one way to accept the absolute truth that you are already enough. The person who is trying their best (and not hurting themselves or anyone else) is *always* enough.

What's meant for you will always be there. You know what will also always be there? You. Yourself. You deserve to plant all the seeds. You don't need to let the fear of rejection stop you from playing in the wonderful field of daisies that is having a crush.

Bravey Notes

- Any circumstance can be viewed with either pessimism or optimism—the choice is yours.

- All great things begin with potential, and it takes bravery to believe in potential.

- It's normal to be afraid of getting rejected. But don't let that stop you from trying! You can't control how someone else will feel about you—you *can* decide to try your best and be honest anyway.

headed to the moon
not now but soon

MY PAL, PAIN

Braveys: Whatever challenging feelings you're holding right now, I promise they are not forever. This is both a good thing *and* a hard thing. It's hard because sometimes, we feel amazing and we never want that to change. Wouldn't it be awesome for life to always feel as exciting as it does when you go to school on a Friday knowing you're sleeping over at your best friend's house that night? But that isn't the way life works. Time always carries us forward, and it can be sad to watch good things fade and change. But this also means that painful feelings we have—feeling angry with a friend, feeling heartbroken over a breakup, feeling devastated for not getting a part in the school play, or any of the other million painful things that happen as we grow up—those feelings will fade and change, too. Pain today will not be the same pain tomorrow.

It can be hard, though, to remember this perspective when you're in the middle of something painful, sad, or otherwise hard. Because when you're in the thick of it, it feels like the bad feelings will last forever. When you've just been dumped, it's impossible to imagine ever feeling better. Pain is part of life and it can't be avoided—but that's okay, because just like in running, rough patches don't last forever. If we hang in there and keep moving forward, we *will* feel better.

I learned this for myself when I began running more seriously. To run a race, and especially to qualify for the Olympics, it is important to become a master of pain. At the Olympics, I ran the 10,000 meters—twenty-five laps, the longest race on the track. It's a grueling combination of endurance running and speed. It's a test of pain tolerance and mental toughness as much as of athletic ability. How much are you willing to suffer?

Throughout my career as an athlete, I've come to trust that I can exert myself to my absolute physical limit, and I will (most likely) not die. Deep down, I know the difference between athletic pain, which is good pain, and other kinds of pain, bad pain. Whatever pain I feel while I'm wearing running shoes can never be as bad as the things I had seen my mom do. Bad pain is scary; good pain just hurts.

But just because I have a high tolerance for pain doesn't mean I enjoy it. In middle and high school, I dreaded every single race. Not because I was anxious about racing well, but because I was terrified of the pain that came with it. I had a very specific daydream that I would entertain before every race: an alien spaceship would land in the middle of the track right before the starting gun and I would get to go home. Nobody could ever make us run after such a dramatic extraterrestrial disruption. But no matter how much I fantasized, the Martians never came and the starting gun always fired— followed by the inevitable onset of pain. The salt-sweat chafing in my armpits and thighs, the swarming ant farm in my legs and stomach, the stinging in my eyes as sweat mixed with sunscreen.

Even when I won, my joy at finishing a race was tainted by the trauma of the pain I had just experienced. I would stomp directly from the finish line over to my dad, who I remember as having a camera for a nose, and report to him that seriously, this race could have killed me, and I simply could *not* go through this again. My dad would say the same thing every time: "It's okay, Lex."

* * *

When I went to college and started training to compete at the Division 1 level, intense pain became part of my daily routine. Every morning I woke up dreading the inevitable pain to come, and by the time practice started, I felt mentally drained. It became clear that if I wanted to survive as a college runner, I needed to develop a technique to manage my fears about pain. I could no longer afford to spend the days leading up to workouts and races steeped in anxiety. Negative thinking drains energy, and I needed all the energy I had to keep up with my new teammates. Pain and I had to come to a new understanding.

I thought back to middle school when I got into a fight with this girl I really didn't get along with. When our teacher finally intervened, she quarantined us in a room called "the pod" for an hour to figure things out, just us two eleven-year-olds. My adversary and I spent a good forty-five minutes in silence, glaring at each other from under our unibrows. But in the end we agreed that while we didn't want or need to be friends, we could be civil for both our sakes. I resolved to be similarly civil with pain. Before my races and big workouts, I worked on consciously shifting my mental energy from dreading upcoming pain to simply recognizing that the pain would always show up no matter what, and even though I utterly despised it, I should try to greet it politely like a guest at a dinner party and be fully prepared to open the door when it knocks. Sometimes pain arrives slowly, like butter melting on toast. Or it can be quick, like butter hitting a very hot pan. Whichever variety of pain I'm getting, I know it is coming and I am prepared to handle it gracefully. *Pain* does not have to equal *suffering*. Pain is a sensation; suffering is a mindset.

The next step was to teach myself to manage the pain once it arrived. Visualization became my most powerful tool: I learned to anticipate which parts of a race would be the most grueling, either by studying the course beforehand or by talking to people who had run the race before. In the days leading up to the race, while jogging, cutting my nails, or scrambling eggs, I'd visualize an Alexi-inside-my-head approaching a specific painful moment along the course and pushing through the rough patch with composure, strength, and even beauty. When I actually faced the challenge in the race, I knew the pain was coming—and, most crucially, I had already made the decision to persevere.

I also discovered using physical triggers, *playable actions,* as a tool to help my mind overcome the anxiety associated with the onset of pain. For example: "When the pain hits after the third mile, remember to shake your arms out and drop your shoulders." Or even something as simple as: "When it hurts, force yourself to smile." By converting a mental struggle into an actionable objective, internal battles felt less elusive and more grounded. It's much easier to tell myself to move my arms than it is to tell myself to "feel better."

After I finished school, I started running professionally with my eye on competing in the Olympics. Thrust into this new world of elite runners, I had a surprising realization: my competitors were all experiencing pain, too. I idolized pro runners when I was growing up, and I assumed that these mythical creatures must have figured *something* out about pain that I hadn't. There's no way that these professionals hurt as much as I did. But now that I was up close to this new tier of athlete, I saw that I wasn't the only one struggling. As it turns out, running hurts for everyone.

Everyone has their own method for managing pain. Some runners wear their pain openly while others hide it very well. But in the same way that it's usually unhelpful to compare my life to how other people's lives look on their Instagram feeds, I had to stop comparing myself to how other people in my races looked. Looks can be deceiving, and more often than not, we try to show only the most glamorous parts of ourselves. But it's important to remember that exterior glamour is never the full picture. Imagine it like this: every person is a planet. Our planet's core is who we truly are, but the world only sees our outer surface. Ideally, how the world sees us and how we feel and see ourselves are one and the same, but the most important thing is that we acknowledge our core, deep inside our planet-selves—that's where our true feelings and self exist. And understand that everyone else has a core inside them, too.

I remember in one of my first competitions after college, I found myself running side by side with an accomplished Olympian who maintained a calm face and strong posture despite our grueling pace. I felt intimidated—was this woman not in pain? But then halfway through the race, she suddenly fell behind the pace and completely dropped back, seemingly out of the blue. I'd been so sure that her steady breathing meant that I was alone in my suffering, when in truth she must have been feeling even more pain than I was. Without a doubt, I learned that day that pain is the one thing my competitors and I definitely have in common.

My deeper understanding of physical pain has helped me cope with emotional pain, too. First of all, I know that pain shows up differently for each person and I can never tell just how much somebody else might be hurting. I also understand that whenever I feel bad, I'm probably not alone. And I also know that however badly I'm hurting in this current moment, it will not last forever.

I remember being heartbroken when my high school boyfriend and I broke up after I graduated and moved across the country to college. There's something uniquely tender about high school heartbreak that makes it especially painful—it's relentless and all-consuming, like when a baby is crying and crying and doesn't stop for hours. Its entire world is tears. That's what high school heartbreak feels like. I felt so sad and lonely that I thought maybe I had made a mistake by going to Dartmouth, a college in New Hampshire, instead of California, and I even started filling out paperwork to transfer to another school closer to home. Luckily my dad encouraged me to stay just a little while longer and finish my freshman year—and sure enough, as the months passed, I started feeling better and came to love Dartmouth.

I know that when your heart is broken or you're running a tough workout or going through any really hard thing, pain feels like a permanent state. It *is* real. But it's also helpful and important to remind yourself that time can and will change your reality. And when it comes to making decisions like switching schools or dropping out of a race early or any other decisions in life we make to avoid pain, it's helpful to remember that how you feel at first isn't necessarily how you'll feel forever.

All pain, whether it's the physical kind you feel during a race or the emotional kind you feel in your heart, gets better with time. Just remember: all marshmallows, when squeezed, can reinflate eventually.

Bravey Notes

- When you are about to embark on something that might be painful, mentally or physically, you can anticipate the pain and visualize yourself persevering. This allows you to be better equipped when the pain arrives. In this way, you are befriending pain.

- Pain today will not be the same tomorrow. Whether it's the physical pain of a tough race or pain that's more emotional, no bad feeling lasts forever. Pain is part of life and it cannot be avoided—but know that if you hang in there and keep moving forward, things *will* change.

grit is what's left over when nothing's left.

THE RULE OF THIRDS

Good coaches give workouts that will change your body. The best coaches give advice that will change your life.

My Olympic coach, Coach Ian, knew when to hold me accountable and when to push me harder, and he also knew when to listen to my complaints and evaluate if something was truly wrong. There were days that he made me take my watch off and continue the workout without obsessing over pace, and there were days when he'd look me in the eye and tell me this was a workout where I needed to suck it up and hit the pace no matter how much it hurt because he knew I could. And then there were days when he saw that I just needed to step off the track and go home.

One day, after a rough workout, I was beating myself

up because I couldn't hit the pace I should have. I felt frustrated and even a little bit afraid, since the Olympics were just around the corner. I thought my slow workout meant that I was failing. But then Coach Ian gave me the best advice I've ever gotten: It's called *the Rule of Thirds.* When you're chasing a big goal, you're supposed to feel good a third of the time, okay a third of the time, and crappy a third of the time. If the ratio is off and you feel good all the time, then you're not pushing yourself enough. Likewise, if you feel bad all the time, then you might be fatigued and need to dial things back.

What is crucial is to give 100 percent of what you have every day, whether it's 100 percent of crap or 100 percent of gold. You acknowledge the day and move on to the next. You're not trying to ignore how you feel every day; instead, you're trying to *observe* how you feel. You're trying to take a more zoomed-out perspective of your journey.

Learning the Rule of Thirds was life-changing for me, not only as an athlete but also as a creative, as someone in a relationship, and as a person in general, because it made me believe in the days that didn't feel great. It also helped me accept that losing is okay. In fact, losing is an ingredient of winning: along the way to being good enough at something, you will inevitably lose. How we label an experience can completely change how we perceive it. Instead of beating myself up about bad days, I relished them, knowing that even those days were an important part of the process. The hard days just meant that I was chasing a dream.

Bravey Notes

- The Rule of Thirds says that when you're chasing a big dream, you can expect to feel good one-third of the time, okay one-third of the time, and crappy one-third of the time. If the ratio feels off, that's an indication to pause and evaluate.

- You won't be able to bring your A game to every workout, test, or other big event. That's okay. What's important is to bring 100 percent of what you do have every day—you can appreciate and believe in the hard days just as much as the good days.

all i want
is to give it
all i got.

THE OLYMPICS

The Olympics, and especially the Olympic Vil-lage in Rio de Janeiro, Brazil, felt like a giant summer camp that brought the world's most athletic bodies and minds together in one place. And, like the first day of camp, I arrived feeling nervous. But instead of worrying about whether I'd packed the right kind of sandals, here it felt like my entire life's work was at stake. I wanted my race to go well, but in a more zoomed-out sense, I wanted very badly for my entire *Olympic experience* to go well. I knew from my coaches and mentors that the Olympics can be everything you imagined or they can fall short of your expectations. It's like meeting a celebrity that you've looked up to for your entire life. If you've always pictured them as this perfect dreamlike being, there's no way they can ever live up to your imaginary ideals. Disappointment is inevitable unless you meet them as they are.

When I arrived in the Olympic Village, the first thing I noticed were the rows of tall, balconied apartment buildings. Every building (except the Team USA building, which opts to be low-key) was covered in flags from the country of the athletes living there—China, Qatar, Czech Republic. The Australian building even had a life-size kangaroo statue outside. Because of my Greek heritage, I was competing for Greece, and my team shared a building with Croatia, Algeria, and Ethiopia, among others. Upon entering our building, the first thing I noticed was a clique of Croatian and Algerian coaches smoking cigarettes and jovially watching the Games on television from beanbag chairs while techno music thumped loudly from a portable speaker. I accepted this reality with what I can only describe as a new-summer-camp smile plastered to my face—the smile you wear when you're overwhelmed, excited, and scared all at once. It's a disarming moment when you realize that you are not fully in control; you're plopped into a new environment that you cannot change.

For elite athletes, especially endurance athletes, control is extremely important. Our sleeping environment, our meals, and even how we spend our downtime are all carefully calibrated and controlled. Now that I was in the Olympic Village, I had to smile politely and accept the fact that unless I wanted to confront an entire horde of strange coaches from Eastern Europe, there *would* be techno music loudly playing in the lobby at all hours of the day and night. It felt like a crossroads moment: either I could try to hold tight to my idea of how things *should* be, or I could let go and embrace this new reality. That is the choice all Olympians must make: to try to sterilize the experience and treat it like any other competition, or to embrace it as something totally special and different. I knew that I could either let the Olympic chaos crush me or I could make it fuel me. So I decided to wear my new-summer-camp smile like a Bravey badge, and I went upstairs to find my room.

I had four suitemates, all of whom were on totally different eating and sleeping schedules. I was the only one who brought the proper power outlet adapter, and thus this tiny object was in high demand by suitemates wanting to charge their phones or straighten their hair. I didn't grow up with sisters, and suddenly I had four. It was fun but overwhelming. I retreated to my bedroom when it felt like too much, wrapping myself in my special Olympic-themed comforter. The comforters at every Olympics are designed with unique colors and graphics reflective of that particular Games' aesthetic. At the end of the Games, every athlete takes their comforter home—mine took up half a suitcase and I will treasure it forever.

Like a summer camp, the Olympic Village had a uniform. Athletes wore their full national team uniforms at all times—this was a requirement enforced by every national team's leadership. Each uniform had multiple components—sweats, warm-ups, T-shirts, shoes, the works—and each country's uniform had its own distinct look. Italy's uniforms were designed by Armani. France's, Lacoste. Sweden's, H&M. The Slovakians' sweats had colorful squiggly circles and squares printed on them. The Greek uniform was mostly Mediterranean blue, and I even got a Greek fanny pack. My favorite item was my rain jacket, blue with tiny white Greek keys printed all over it. My uniform was gigantic on me—the smallest item I had was a T-shirt that fell below my knees. But despite the size mismatch, when I wore my uniform, I felt like I belonged in this village of athletes. It felt like I had arrived.

* * *

I never felt any negative external pressure to perform well in my race, but I desperately wanted it to go well. Not just for my own sake but also because I was the first female distance runner for Greece *ever* to make it to the

Olympics in the 10,000 meters—nobody had run the qualifying time before. The Greeks have particularly strong national pride when it comes to the Olympics—after all, Greece is where it all began—and it is always the first country to enter the Olympic Stadium during the opening ceremony in the Parade of Nations.

As a dual citizen of the United States and Greece, I could have stated my athletic allegiance to either country, but competing for Greece gave me the opportunity to make a larger impact with my performance. I will always remember when I went to my first training camp in rural Greece. A group of young girls who were there to watch the boys play soccer instead fixated on me running around the perimeter of the field. They asked why I looked strong "like a boy" and could hardly believe it when I told them that I was an athlete—they had never been exposed to female athletes who looked like me before. A good result in my race, now just a few days away, would make big waves in Greece and mean so much to so many people. It might even spark a fledgling Olympic dream for a young girl who would never have considered sports otherwise, and that meant the most to me.

To pass the time, I spent an inordinate number of hours in the athlete village dining hall, a colossal white structure two football fields long that resembled a holiday cake roll. There were giant food stations that boasted tubs of quail eggs, passion fruit, and countless prepared foods and condiments from cuisines around the world. I learned the hard way that the giant bucket of yellowish stuff next to the cold cuts was not honey mustard, it was dulce de leche. I've never gotten over the novelty of always having a hot meal ready for me—and the dining hall was full of novelties. It didn't feel real; it felt like an escape from my real life. But then I remembered: *every part of my life is my real life.*

The dining hall was open twenty-four hours a day, and it was the best place to people-watch. All of our sports and countries were different, but everybody has to eat. Whenever I was feeling nervous or lonely, the dining hall was where I'd go. I think it is nice to be around other heartbeats even if they don't speak your language and even if they don't notice you're there, sitting alone, two seats over, observing how differently they use their fork and knife. I craved the backdrop of people more than I craved actual interaction with them.

My favorite game to play in the dining hall to distract myself from my own nerves was to guess an athlete's sport by looking at them. There were so many different shapes and sizes of people, and I tried to guess their sport by the look of their body or by the kind of crew they were rolling with. A giant posse meant it might be a team sport—if all the same gender, then even more likely—

which narrowed things down. But my guessing game didn't stop at what sport someone might play. That was just the beginning of my speculative rabbit hole. I liked to imagine how people lived their life outside of the Olympic Village. I drew conclusions about people based on how they walked and carried themselves. Some athletes navigated the dining hall carefully, slowly, and with their heads down. That meant they might be new or nervous, which made me feel better; even if I was nervous, at least I was not alone.

But the dining hall wasn't only filled with the nervous head-down, hood-up types. There were also the confident, social-looking athletes—the boisterous, gregarious types, often found in packs with their team. It's easier to feel confident when you have your team with you—sometimes, teams of athletes would burst into national chants or cheers, especially after a big competition, and everyone nearby would smile and watch, like when the waiters all gather around someone's table in a restaurant to sing "Happy Birthday."

But the athletes who really caught my eye were the ones who projected confidence even when they were alone. If someone was basically gliding about the dining hall, summoning their burger and their noodles onto the plate like a god, then I guessed they had been to the Olympics before and were coming from a place of experience and knowledge. These people made me feel hopeful simply because I was occupying the same rarified space as them—I'd see how confident they looked and I'd tell myself that I had earned my spot here just like them, so maybe I should let myself feel confident like them, too. I am always fishing for ways to feel more confident and at home in places where I'm nervous. The truth is, playing this guessing game about other people's lives was a way to craft a narrative that helped me relate to each person I saw. It helped me convince myself that I fit in. The more I was able to see myself in my peers, the more I felt a part of the Olympics, and the more I felt capable of doing something great there.

* * *

Before my 10,000-meter race at the track stadium, there was pandemonium behind the scenes. Performing well was just as much about surviving the journey to the start line as it was about the race itself. Dozens of races needed to go off exactly at their scheduled times, without exception—after all, each race was the most important race in its athletes' lives. Amid the endless serpentine hallways through the track stadium's backstage, it seemed impossible that my competitors and I would get to where we needed to be without losing our hip numbers, losing our way, and losing our lunch.

There's a saying that races are won and lost in the warm-up areas, and it's true. Before a race, it is easier to lose confidence than to gain it. I could tell that some of my competitors left their confidence on the warm-up field by the way they hung their heads, like the bobbleheads my dad obsessively collected from baseball games. I remember he would grab my hand and navigate me through the crowds and up the switchback ramps at the San Francisco Giants' stadium, half a step too swift for my nine-year-old legs. As I navigated the labyrinthine tunnels beneath the Olympic track stadium, my mind took me to the Giants' stadium back home. There's a funny thing about stadium hallways: they all smell the same.

My competitors and I finally arrived in the first of two call rooms where we were to be processed ahead of the race. In the first call room, we had our equipment checked—my competitors and I exchanged nervous looks while taking out our special track spikes, which are basically ballet slippers with nails underneath, and lacing them up anxiously. I saw different shoe-tying techniques all around me, and for a moment I questioned my own lacing methods, but I knew better than to change anything that specific on race day.

Through a crack in the door I could see into the main stadium hallway where spectators wandered between events, buying popcorn and commemorative T-shirts.

The people with their ice creams and hot dogs were completely unaware that thirty-seven restless athletes were behind a thin wall just a few feet away. I closed my eyes to quiet my mind, but I was interrupted by a poke from a lady who handed me my official race bib and instructed me on how to fasten it to my uniform. She had the eyes of someone who had seen countless anxious athletes before me: no-nonsense, but also thoughtful and caring beneath her strict demeanor. She was going to instruct but not help, like a mother bird firmly but lovingly throwing her chick out of the nest.

After fifteen endless minutes in the first call room, a tall man in a sweat-drenched white cotton shirt told us it was time to move to the second call room. He had the enthusiasm of a parent who does not want to be a chaperone on a school field trip. As we all walked to the next room, my mind switched back and forth between feeling ready and feeling wholly unprepared for the task ahead.

In the second call room, I adjusted my shoes one last time. I have an irrational fear of losing a shoe mid-race, and I've come to accept that no amount of experience or mental fortitude will soothe it. So I just tie my shoes insanely tight before a race so there's no room for fear in my feet, and I leave it at that.

The tall sweaty man in the white cotton shirt yelled: "Everybody take your clothes off! Uniforms only! Everybody! Clothes! Off! Now! GIRLS!" Each of us took off our sweats until we were down to just race buns (basically underwear that we wear to race), spandex, and track spikes.

Then the man gathered us and told us it was time to test the special timing chips implanted in our race bibs. We were instructed to scurry across a little timing test mat one by one. If the mat beeped, it meant our timing chip was activated. This was all communicated by physical pantomime, since there were so many language barriers among the thirty-seven athletes, which meant this sweaty man had to demonstrate by bounding across the little mat himself.

One by one, like a group of trained circus lions, we leapt across the timing mat. What we weren't told was that we could not go back—the mat was a one-way ticket to the trackside corral, the final pre-race holding area. A wave of panic rippled through my competitors in the corral, as nobody had thought to bring their water bottles across the mat to the other side. Nobody, that is, except for me.

Just moments ago I had been a relatively low-profile young athlete among my thirty-six competitors, but suddenly I became *The One with the Water*. If I'd wanted to I could have hoarded this water like a secret power that only I controlled. But then a voice next to me piped up: "Can I have a sip?" It was Almaz Ayana, the runner from Ethiopia who went on to break the world record during our 10,000-meter race.

I hesitated for a moment. It would have been entirely fair and within my rights to turn everyone else's lack of water into an advantage for myself. A younger me might have felt this was an opportunity to get private payback for the feeling of "lack" I had growing up. But then I considered all the incredible generosity that people have shown me throughout my life—and I grew up before my own eyes as I watched myself hand my water bottle to Almaz. This happens sometimes, where you notice yourself subtly but meaningfully surpassing your own expectations. And in that moment, you redefine who you are for yourself. I am now someone who shares. Growing up isn't always passive and gradual; sometimes it can be active and very sudden. Almaz smiled at me, took a healthy sip of my water, and then passed it on to the next girl. In this moment, I felt better for each drop of water shared than I would have for each drop of water hoarded. I couldn't help but think: All of these women want to kick your butt in this race, but all of them are basically good. It's not really us against each other, it's us against the whole world, all those popcorn and hot-dog people in the stands and the millions of others watching from their couches. We're all about to go do this wild dance together.

Then, quite suddenly, the corral door opened and we walked out onto the bright track. After a lifetime of preparing, the moment was finally here. I took a few sprints up and down the straightaway while television cameras hovered above me like curious hummingbirds. I looked into one of the cameras and waved, picturing my grandparents on the other side of the lens. It was the same feeling as being backstage in one of my elementary school plays right before the curtain comes up. Running is also a performance: We go onto a stage in a costume and we are the spectacle. We even wear makeup. On race day I always wear far more makeup than I ever do in real life, because this is a performance and it's supposed to feel special. But with running, the biggest performance isn't what the audience sees—it's what goes on inside your own mind. It's an inward performance: How much pain can I handle today? For me, putting on race-day makeup isn't about how the world sees me; it's about how I see myself. My race-day makeup symbolizes that this day is unique. It means that I am about to try something brave.

After a few moments the cameras pulled back and a hush settled over the stadium. I walked to the start line, took my position, and waited. A breath of silence, and then . . . POP! The starting gun fired and we took off running. All of us were trying to run faster than we ever had before. This was it, our Olympic race. Everything in our lives before had led to this point.

* * *

My coach had given me a specific pace to run for the majority of the race, and I stuck to our plan. I understood that I would begin in the far back of the pack but that it would pay off in the end. This was absolutely the case, as I slowly picked off one girl and then another, and another. I felt confident, controlled, and joyful. When you are truly prepared for a race it can feel like you're almost watching yourself run while you run. I felt at home among my newfound sisters. We were all in this together.

Then the girl behind me kicked me in the heel and stepped on the back of my shoe. Then she kicked my heel again. And AGAIN. When something like this happens once, it's an accident. Twice, okay. But three or four times and we have problems. That's when I remembered that this was not a kumbaya campfire, this was a race, and I was here to compete.

The 10k is a race about *endurance,* so generally it's not a matter of who runs away with it early but more about who is left at the end. I was now about halfway through the race, at which point the goal is to hang in there and not do anything crazy, just conserve energy for the climactic final lap. I kept telling myself to "stay."

But then there came the moment when the hurt set in. Every race hurts, no matter what. If anybody tells you otherwise they're either lying or they simply don't try hard enough. Normally when the hurt sets in I tuck my head down, grit my teeth, and force myself to smile. Then I thought about my family somewhere in the audience and all the ups and downs they had weathered during my journey to get here. I thought about how if the pain overcame me and I really did die right then and there, it was okay because there was nothing else I'd rather be doing.

As I ditched the heel-kicker and approached the final lap, running faster than I ever had, I realized that this wasn't really about me versus *her*—meaning any individual girl in my race—nor was this about me versus the world at large. It was about *me versus me,* just like in middle school, running as fast as I can and then some. It was about enjoying the results of my hard work and all the help I got from the people I love. My mental fitness and physical fitness were completely in sync, peaking simultaneously. It felt like the steep climb that began when I was a freshman at Dartmouth, with the countless days of pain and commitment, had culminated in this one moment of perfect harmony. "Me versus me" doesn't do this feeling justice either—it's not a *versus*. It's me *within* me and me *outside* of me. I was running around the track while looking at a miniature diorama version of myself running around the track, and this image repeated in my heart to infinity. It felt like my mind could tell my body to do anything and it would do it. Some people call this flow, but I call it bliss.

* * *

When you cross the finish line at the Olympics, there is no dad or boyfriend or coach to catch you. They are somewhere beyond the barricade of security fences. The people who catch you are the women you just raced, all of you wobbly and confused and happy and sad at the same time, overwhelmed that this thing you've held in your mind forever has finally happened.

I stood on the track and waited for the last runner to finish. I saw my results go up on the giant jumbotron: I ran 31:36, shattering my personal best and setting a new Greek national record. I felt elated; I had done my absolute best. I felt like an Olympian. When you finish a race like this, it is emotional. You hold so many feelings at once. You probably cry. I cried. I cried because it was the end of something and the beginning of something else.

After the race, when the dust settled and I was alone in my twin bed in my Olympic Village dorm later that night, I felt uneasy. I didn't want my Olympic experience to be over. Luckily, I still had two whole weeks left before the closing ceremony. That was two more weeks at the Olympics before I'd have to pack my bags and return to the real world.

I was aware that each second at the Games was precious. I wanted to soak up everything, like a sponge cake where the syrupy glaze saturates each morsel, crumb, and divot. I wanted the full experience. I had a vague inkling that maybe I'd try again for the next Olympics, but I had seen enough star athletes end their careers unexpectedly early to know and fully appreciate that this Olympic opportunity might come only once in my lifetime. I began to understand why it is important to take the opportunities we have in life when we get them, because only yesterday and today are for sure.

Soon the closing ceremony was just one day away. It felt exactly like the last day of summer camp: Everyone knows this is the last day to have fun before the buses come to whisk us back to the abyss of the real world. I couldn't help but feel nervous that I had somehow not soaked it all in enough.

During this last day, when I was wandering the village alone with my thoughts and frankly feeling a bit sorry for myself, I came across the beauty salon. I had heard that there was a free exclusive salon for Olympic athletes. But the beauty salon puzzled me: Why would anyone want to get a makeover at the Olympics? I always wear makeup to the starting line, but as it is with most obsessive athletes, this is a ritual I perform on myself. Still, the salon beckoned to me—and in the spirit of experiencing all the Olympics have to offer, I decided to partake.

I ventured inside. A man at the front desk took one look at me and sprang out of his chair as if he could sense that I hadn't had my hair or makeup done in a salon in a very, *very* long time. He introduced himself as Kiko and told me that he would make me look like Lady Gaga. Before Kiko would handle my hair with his own hands, though, he asked me to comb it. He suspected that this was a battle best handled by me. I took the brush and began ripping through the many knots that dotted my head like holiday lights. I forced the brush from scalp to tip like a freight train bursting through piles of snow on the tracks. If a chunk of hair wasn't cooperating, it was torn out.

"No! No, no, no." Kiko stopped me. "Didn't anybody ever teach you?" I reached into the depths of my earliest memories to recall the moment when someone surely taught me how to properly brush my hair, but came up with nothing. I shook my head no. Nobody had ever taught me. It reminded me of the time in college when, during a class on "civic skills training"—I'm oversimplifying here, but it's basically a class where students learn how to present themselves and interact with people in a professional way—the professor told me in front of the whole class that I "didn't know how to walk like a lady." I remember her expression as some mix of harshness, amusement, and disappointment.

But Kiko's face was so tender and forgiving, it was as if he had just found an abandoned kitten in a cardboard box. "Like this," he said, and he delicately selected a lock of hair from the forest atop my head and separated it from the rest. Then, beginning at the bottom, not the root, he gently nudged the brush over and over again into the tangle.

"Here, you try," Kiko told me tenderly, extending the brush. I did my best to imitate his movements. I was not used to being gentle and kind to myself in this way. But in general, I took to his method. I liked the way it made me feel calm and in control of myself, and I liked how not fighting so hard actually got me closer to my goal. When we were done with brushing, I looked like a kitten but felt like a lion. Then Kiko took over the project entirely. He spun me away from the mirror so I could no longer see myself—this way, the transformation would be more dramatic.

He matted my hair down with a combination of mousse and hair spray. Then he wiped my face clean and covered it with powder. I still wasn't allowed to see myself, but I could see the makeup palette Kiko held: an out-of-focus mound of purple dust. He told me with utter confidence that my color was purple and that I should try to wear purple as often as possible.

While hair spray and purple eye shadow are not the first tools I personally reach for when trying to look my best, Kiko had a clear vision for me in a moment when I did not have one for myself. He put thought into me, and that mattered. It made me feel *paid-attention-to*. There are two ways to be paid-attention-to: there is the way where people are judging you, which can make you feel bad, and then there is this way where someone makes you feel special and good. The good kind of attention is filled with what I can only describe as dedication, thoughtfulness, and love. Once we are too old to have a mom or big sister pay attention to us on a daily basis, it is usually up to us to pay attention to ourselves in this loving way. But it is different when the attention comes from us versus when it comes from someone else. Both are important. In this moment, Kiko gave all his attention to me. His calmness and confidence jumped from his hands through my hair and into my heart. It made me feel good. Feeling good is important. It feels like the start of something great.

When he was done, Kiko held a mirror up so I could get a good look at myself: his creation. I felt like a walking work of art. It wasn't a look I'd wear every day, but this was not every day. This was special. It felt like an encapsulation of my Olympic experience, where I was thrust into an environment that was completely outside of my comfort zone—but it was okay, because I embraced and even celebrated the discomfort. If I had held too tight to the old routines and comforts that I typically rely on before a race, my Olympic experience would have slipped through my fingers like an ice cube. I'm glad I didn't. The purple eye shadow Kiko gave me was the greatest. I felt ready to face the closing ceremony the next day, like the big dance on the last night of camp. I realized that it was okay to be nervous about the Olympics ending. Nerves are cousin to excitement, and excitement is cousin to gratitude. Pay attention to your nerves: if you feel nervous, it's a sign that a Very Big Thing is unfolding. Be nervous for how good that thing can be.

Bravey Notes

- When you're going to a new place or a big event, it might feel scary to be out of your normal routine, but it can also be fun to recognize the experience as something special and embrace what makes it different.

- It's okay to feel nervous when you're about to do a very big thing—nerves are cousin to excitement. Nerves mean you care.

- Competition doesn't have to be antagonistic; there can also be camaraderie between competitors. Sports are about doing your personal best.

not your first
not your last
enjoy your now
now will go fast

DEPRESSION

When it began, it came in the form of sleep-lessness.

I began to lose sleep shortly after returning from Rio. It's not uncommon for Olympians to feel a post-Olympic depression, however mild or severe. It makes sense: you've worked your whole life toward this exceptionally challenging and singular goal, and then it happens, and suddenly it's over. Up until this point, the Olympics are your rising and setting sun. You never think about life after the Olympics because if you thought about the moment after, you might not get there in the first place. You put everything you have into *getting there,* into climbing the mountain, but we never think about how to come down safely. So when it is over, however well it goes, the feeling is sharp and disorienting. You're stuck on top of this peak with no path down. The descent is more dangerous than the ascent. I've spoken with athletes who won gold medals and others who had to drop out of their race, and no matter how someone performed, that post-Olympic dip is similar. It happens in non-Olympic life, too. Anyone can feel a dip after any big milestone is over, whether it's school graduation or even just the day after your birthday.

But I didn't have any vocabulary or frame of reference to understand this. I went into it completely unaware. This was before mental health awareness had entered our culture in a mainstream way; before "post-Olympic depression" was even a term that people used regularly.

In mild forms, post-Olympic depression is like a ledge. For me, it was a cliff. The healthy thing to do after the Olympics ended would have been to take a vacation, or at least a mental break, to give myself time to absorb the enormity of what I had just experienced, to celebrate, and *then* start to plan my next steps with a clear mind and fresh perspective. I needed to climb down the mountain, to *decompress*, and then charge my next adventure. But instead I felt I needed to keep my momentum going, so when I got back home from the Games, I continued my training without pause.

Why did I feel this need to keep going without a break? I think, deep down, it's because I felt like external accomplishments proved to the world—and, most importantly, to myself—that I was *doing okay*. Despite growing up without my mom, I survived and thrived. Of course, I didn't know this at the time. All I knew was that I was fueled by dedication bordering on desperation to be the very best athlete I could be. I saw the best path to happiness as chasing external success, the Olympics being the pinnacle of what I could hope to achieve. I think I thought, without realizing it, that once I became the greatest, no one would ever leave me again. But this was not a healthy mindset, to place so much of my *inner* well-being on the outcome of an *external* event. It's okay and wonderful to chase big goals, but it's important to know that our goals don't define us—and they can't fix us, either. Happiness needs to come from inside. We are all allowed to be happy and feel *good enough* simply because we exist. That's the wonderful part about being human. But I didn't understand that yet.

Here's what happens when you depend on external goals for your inner happiness: nothing you accomplish is ever enough. You always scramble ahead, searching for the next goal and the next and the next. So that's what I did. Instead of feeling proud of what I had achieved at the Olympics, I set my sights on the next big athletic milestone I could think of: racing my first marathon. I parted ways with my coach and moved from Eugene, Oregon, to a high-altitude training camp in the mountain town of

Mammoth Lakes, California. I was also between creative projects—my movie, *Tracktown,* had just come out—and every minute that I wasn't running, I was at my computer scrambling to come up with new creative ideas. I felt more and more like my work was motivated by running away from failure instead of running toward opportunity. And being motivated by fear of failure is the surest way to fail, especially in the athletic and creative worlds. When fear is your primary motivation, you become fueled by *desperation* rather than *passion.* Desperation and passion are opposite ends of the same spectrum, but while passion is a magnetic force that attracts success and inspires people, desperation does the opposite.

Any one of those big changes—switching coaches, trying a new event, moving to a new town, starting a new creative project—is a major milestone that takes time to adjust to. If I had taken some time off and properly recovered after the Olympics, I might have had a healthier perspective and given myself more space to slowly make those big shifts in my life. But I did it all at once. Some part of me, deep down, knew I was being reckless. I had a constant feeling of unease—which, over time, blossomed into anxiety. These changes were more than I could bear. My rational brain spiraled away down a drain in the back of my mind, and fear crawled up to take its place. I stopped sleeping.

***

For some people depression comes on slowly, but for me, it happened all at once. My psychiatrist later described it like this: you are walking along and then suddenly you stumble and fall off a cliff. There is not a perfect equation for what causes someone to get clinical depression. It's highly individual, and there are different thresholds for different people. But I wouldn't meet my psychiatrist or understand any of this until much later. All I knew at the moment was that I couldn't sleep. Sleep is important, because when we are sleeping, our stress response recalibrates. Our brain reinflates. But instead of sleeping, every night I'd lie in bed frantically trying to figure out what to do next. It felt like I was brushing my brain with a brush whose bristles were made out of fear and anxiety. I'd rake the brush over my brain again and again, never actually accomplishing anything except depriving myself of sleep, until it felt like my whole brain was a knotted tangle of fear. The parts of your brain that make you feel fear are not the same parts of your brain that are capable of rational thought—and it's very easy for the fear center in your brain (the amygdala) to overshadow your thought center (the neocortex). When you're consumed by fear, you can't think straight.

I felt anxious to do anything I could to climb out of this

pit. I feared the worst: both my mom and her brother had died by suicide. That's both kids in her family. As I understand it, their mother—my maternal grandmother—also had struggles with her mental health. With the history of mental illness in my family, I am obligated to tick the box about depression every time I go to the doctor. I am reminded of it constantly. I've always been afraid there is an invisible timer in my head that will one day run out and I will become like my mom, and I was terrified that I was now on a collision course with a destiny that I was desperate to avoid. I thought that if I could handle the situation at hand, I could outrun the darkness that was threatening to engulf me.

My sleeplessness grew worse as nine hours of sleep per night gradually shrank to one, if I was lucky. My mind would not shut off. It felt like my entire *life* was at stake; I was stewing in fear and anxiety every day. It would have been wise to seek help the minute I began having these unhealthy feelings, but that's not what I did. I wasn't mature enough to see beyond my own fear and resentment toward change. I wandered circles around my apartment alone, searching for sleep like buried treasure, but found none. I commanded myself to sleep, but we all know that's not how it works. That's why it's called *falling asleep,* because it's something we *let* happen, not *make* happen. Sleep requires safety, not desperation. My lack of sleep and increasing anxiety were stifling, and I began to have trouble even thinking straight. I was looking at the world through a kaleidoscope distorted by anxiety and exhaustion. The only time I felt any respite from my horror were brief moments of euphoria when I thought about going to sleep and never waking up. I was happy because I thought I knew what I needed: to disappear. Knowing what you need is a nice feeling, except when you're too sick to think. I felt like I was losing my grip on reality. I was always so good at planning my life and working hard to achieve the goals I set, no matter how lofty, but now I was in a complete free-fall.

The only healthy thing I could have done at that point would have been to stop everything and get help. But back then I stuck to my commitments, even if they were dangerous. I continued to train as hard as ever in Mammoth Lakes, running up to 120 miles a week at 8,000 feet on one hour of sleep per night. That kind of mileage is hard with ten hours of sleep and a nap every day, as I always had done when I took training trips to Mammoth Lakes in the past. You can't run that much mileage without recovering, and sleep is the most important means for the body to bounce back from that level of strain without getting injured.

There was no doubt that my body was breaking down just like my mind. My stress level kept climbing. I later learned that the mind is more susceptible to depression at higher altitudes because there's less oxygen in the air. The combination of anxiety and sleeplessness was the worst feeling I've ever had, like my brain was a searing hot pan. It was untouchable. Sleeplessness turned me into a different person. It didn't allow my brain and body and heart to be on the same page. And when your brain and body and heart are on different pages, it tears you apart like tissue paper. I was so bleary-eyed that I couldn't even see myself anymore. I'd lie in bed for hours, feeling tears slowly crawl down my face like fat lazy bugs. I was a running zombie.

I didn't slow down. If anything, I only sped up and tried to run through it. I trained harder. I tried to continue pushing forward even though something was obviously not right. I didn't ask for help, and I even rejected it, despite being gripped by agonizing anxiety and uncertainty every day. I beat myself up endlessly and blamed myself for ruining my own life. When you are depressed, everything feels like it's your fault. I continued to train hard without sleeping, and sure enough, I developed the first serious injury of my life. My injury was clearly stress related: a partial hamstring tear, easy to develop if you sleep one hour a night and train like an Olympian. Unfortunately, Mammoth Lakes is such a small town that the medical resources were limited. There were no physical therapists available who had experience working with Olympic-level distance runners.

I had an ominous feeling that I had somehow irreparably jeopardized my ability to be a professional athlete. All I wanted to do was curl up in a ball and go back in time to the way things were before. I was convinced that if I could only *go back* and reverse the events of the past few months, I could fix everything. I tried to undo everything I'd done, which should have been another sign I needed help. The minute you start looking backward, when you entertain the idea of trying to unscramble an egg, you need to ask for help. You need to stop moving and deal with yourself at exactly where you are in that moment.

But rather than stop and evaluate, I made fast, flailing moves to save what I saw as my rapidly sinking career. I probably could have corrected course and stopped training to let my hamstring heal, but depression can distort how you see yourself and your place in the world. I thought I needed to be in my old town, with my old coach and my old trainers, running my old trails with my old teammates. I wanted my old everything.

My fiancé Jeremy and I packed up our car with whatever we could fit—like it was an impulsive weekend vacation—and drove thirteen hours from Mammoth back to Eugene. We didn't have a house in Eugene anymore, so we crashed with friends, not knowing how long we would be in town. All of our belongings were now spread among our condo in Mammoth Lakes, a storage unit in Eugene, and the suitcase we kept at whichever friend's place where we were crashing. One week in Eugene became two, became three, became I can't even remember how long, while Jeremy and I bounced between friends' couches, Airbnbs, and house-sitting gigs.

I tried to fold back into my old life, too proud or stubborn to admit anything was wrong. I joined all my old teammates on a training trip to Flagstaff, Arizona. Even though I was injured and even though I wasn't on that team anymore, I insisted on going to the training camp. At some point during the camp, it was my birthday, and I was so sad and miserable that I didn't tell anyone. My teammates and I went to Chipotle for dinner, and I was so out of it that I asked the cashier if my burrito would be free since it was my birthday. That's how my teammates found out it was my birthday. They felt bad, but I felt worse.

From Flagstaff, I flew to Chicago to make an appearance at a big road race in Chicago, a commitment I had made months prior to my injury and depression. I was the reigning champion of the race, having won for the past two years in a row, but now I felt like a shell of that person. Even though I was in no position to be traveling or making a public appearance, I insisted on honoring my commitment to go to the race. I was desperate not to drop out of this event because I felt I needed to continue to do everything I was supposed to be doing. *Supposed to* was another phrase I couldn't let go of—I was supposed to do this and I was supposed to be that—so I kept doing things that helped me appear normal to the outside world, but none of them would help me heal myself. I felt like I was trying to catch all the feathers bursting from a torn pillow. I ended up jogging the race with a random little girl. I tried my best to be there for her during a time when I was not there for myself. Despite being completely terrified and also in severe physical pain, I managed to pull it off. There are articles written about me being a role model that day, and while I am proud to have been a positive presence at the race, it scares me to think about how well I was able to cover up what was really going on inside.

People did not understand what was going on inside my mom's head, either, when she started to lose it. I have been told that nobody knew the extent to which she was sick. We are both brilliant smilers and perpetual over-achievers, and as I understand it, my mom tried until she died. She pretended everything was okay when it wasn't. And now here I was, doing the exact same thing.

I remember swimming in the pool at the Hilton in Chicago after the race; I floated on my back and thought about how I'd messed up my life in a way that I'd never thought possible. I felt *doom*. That was a new feeling for me, the sinking feeling that things are irreversibly bad and will never get better. I wanted to drown.

Floating in the pool and staring into nowhere, I realized that my worst nightmare was coming true: I reminded myself of my mother. I could feel her calling to me the way the Sirens called to Odysseus. I thought back to the old photo album that contains the only pictures I have of my mother, from sometime during her high school years: some of the photos are from her sweet sixteen; others are of former boyfriends, school choir performances and baseball games, and graduation. She was successful, beautiful, and popular. Whenever I looked at the photo album, I felt weird that the smiling girl in the pictures didn't know that she'd one day take her own life. How could she be so happy in this moment and then become something else entirely? When did the switch happen, and could she see it coming?

For my whole life I'd prided myself on how different I was from my mother. I was quite certain that I was above it all, that what happened to her could not happen to me. I had to see myself as different from her for my own survival. But when I thought about seeing her look so genuinely happy as a teenager in the photo album, it scared me. It reminded me of all the photos of myself smiling at the Olympics. I had no idea that just a few months after those photos were taken, my entire life would feel like it was falling apart.

People have told me they did everything they could to help my mom but she was unable to be helped. I started to worry that like her, I was *unhelpable*. When I was younger, I had sympathy for my mother—how sad she must have been! But now I felt *empathy* for her. This is the strongest connection I've ever felt to my mom: when I finally understood what it felt like to want to disappear. I never wanted to get to know her in this way.

I never wanted to actually feel anything approaching what she must have felt. I used to think about all the ways I wanted to live, and now I thought about all the ways I could die. It was so sad, the saddest feeling I've ever experienced. At the same time, this type of understanding is something I think I've craved my whole life. I grew up feeling like everyone else in the world knew my mother better than me: her friends, her teachers, my dad, my brother—everyone. People who knew her would often try to tell me about her—your mom was a good athlete, your mom used to sew—and while I liked learning things about her, it also reminded me how much I didn't know her. But now, in this sick way, I understood her more than anyone else could.

* * *

Growing up, I had no problem asking for help. I spent my whole life unashamedly latching on to mentors and seeking out their expertise. But in those cases, I only felt unknowledgeable or confused, not *crazy*. I'd always been the successful person asking for guidance, not the unstable person asking for rescue. It is hard for a successful person to ask for help in that way. It's dangerous when you decide you must always be "okay" because everyone thinks you are and that's all they've ever known of you. Sometimes the strongest, most successful people haven't developed the muscle that knows when and how to ask for the help they need. I didn't think I needed help. Instead, I tried to get back into a routine in Eugene that somewhat approached the normal life I remembered. It didn't exactly feel like things were getting better, but at least I didn't feel like I was in free-fall anymore. I felt comfortably settled at rock bottom. I was living a ghost version of my old life. I was injured and had no particular goals, but at least I knew where I was sleeping for the foreseeable future. Every day felt like a haze, and I accepted as fact that my life as I knew it was over, irreparably damaged, and now it was my fate to exist in perpetual misery.

One day, my former college teammate and roommate Anne was visiting Eugene from Germany. She had come all the way from Europe and had five precious days to visit the place where she felt most at home, the place where so many of us had found our potential and grown into ourselves. When Anne and I met up, it was immediately clear to her that something was terribly wrong with me. I was able to fake it during my public appearances, but it's hard to fake it with good friends. We went on a walk in the woods where we used to run, and I wasn't even able to talk to her in full sentences. I kept stuttering and then eventually crying. Anne was never one to freak out. It was her calmness that, way back when, helped our team win a National Championship title. I remember Anne calming me down the night before the race—assuring me that I would not let everyone down, as I feared. She told me I would be okay because she knew I would be.

But this time, Anne wasn't sure I was okay. I told her I had ruined my career. I told her I wasn't sleeping. I told her I was injured. I told her that everything was hopeless and that I wished I could go back in time. I told her that I'd walk to the grocery store way more than I needed to and just wander around without buying anything. I didn't tell her that every time I heard a train whistle—trains often passed through Eugene—I'd think about lying on the tracks. The train whistle felt like it was beckoning me. After our walk ended, Anne didn't want to let me be alone. Instead she called Kimber, another friend and former teammate. Even though Anne only had five days to visit Eugene, she and Kimber decided to arrange a mini-trip to Portland to go wedding dress shopping. My wedding was coming up in just a few months—my boyfriend, Jeremy, had proposed to me just before the Olympics—but now, in my depression, wedding dress shopping was not something I could wrap my mind around. Anne and Kimber merrily but calmly drove me the two hours to Portland and ignored my repeated apologies for how much of a downer I was being. They didn't make me feel weird for feeling weird.

When we got to Portland, I told them I didn't feel like trying on dresses anymore and asked if we could just drive the two hours back to Eugene, but they persisted, patiently. Anne and Kimber are just the right amount of stubborn, the amount that you need in your life when you are severely depressed, especially when you don't yet understand that you are severely depressed. I didn't need them to tell me I was crazy or pathetic, I could already feel that myself. And I didn't need them to push me away and tell me to get help, I wasn't ready for that yet. I needed them to let me cry in the car, then buy me a cold-pressed juice, wipe my face, and get me into the fitting room. Friends help you feel dignified even when you do not. Like when I fell in the steeplechase water pit during a practice run the day before a huge race, and Anne jumped in with me just to save me from being embarrassed in front of the rival team's coach, who made a snide comment when he saw me fall. "There, now we're both wet," she said triumphantly. Humiliation cannot survive when a friend is by your side.

I actually ended up finding the skirt I wore to my wedding. The pictures of me trying on the skirt are miserable—I have a photo where I am wearing a gown while holding the complimentary glass of champagne they give you, with a backdrop of other brides-to-be, and I look heartbreakingly sad, like a wilting rose. Now I love that photo because it's a reminder of how good my friends were to me during this terrible time, and when my wedding day eventually came, I was so happy to have that skirt. That's kind of how getting help is when you're in denial about being sick: You don't want it in the moment, but eventually you will be happy you got it.

The best advice I have for anyone who is trying to help a friend in need is: help in the little ways you can, remember it's not personal or about you (any frustration you feel is actually just love), do whatever you can to help them maintain their dignity during this difficult time, and— most importantly—make sure *someone* in a position of responsibility, whether it's a parent or a teacher or a doctor, is keeping an eye on your friend and is ready to step in if necessary.

* * *

Anne knew that throughout all of this, my dad called regularly to make sure I was okay. Since I could not run, I would often talk to him while walking in the woods on my favorite trail ever, a gorgeous winding path through Hendricks Park. In the past, whenever I was feeling down, a run through Hendricks Park would always leave me feeling better. Trail running in the woods is one of my favorite activities. It gives me a different type of joy than road running or racing; it's a joy that touches every sense individually and makes me feel ebullient, present, and connected to the earth. But not anymore. I was not even able to enjoy the misty wet leaves of Eugene flopping lazily over their moss-covered branches. I was weary, like a used tea bag, unable to appreciate ordinary wonderful things. I was really only honest about this with my dad. I was not even honest with my fiancé at that time.

Over the weeks and months since the Olympics had ended, my dad had been there for countless phone calls where I described step by step the unfolding disaster that was my life. He has always been super calm and has been there to listen to me, rock-solid and attentive but never stepping in to save me. He lets me fail and succeed on my own. My dad understands that it is natural and normal for children to struggle and that it's not always productive for a parent to intervene.

But this time was different. Even though I hadn't yet

spoken the words and admitted that I was depressed and needed serious help, he was hearing things that were red flags. Things that might have reminded him of my mother. Unlike Jeremy, who was right there in the thick of it with me and didn't yet fully understand or empathize with what my depression truly meant, my dad could see from afar and knew from experience that something wasn't right. Sometimes it takes a certain kind of distance from a situation to see it clearly, like how you can't stand too close to a Seurat painting and understand what it is. My brother was also concerned for me. Our family has always functioned more like a team than a typical family hierarchy, so when something is wrong, we all know. For the first time, my dad told me I needed *professional help.* He wasn't willing to be a patient ear any longer—he had heard enough and was putting his foot down. I needed to see a doctor.

My dad hardly ever puts his foot down, so when he does, I listen. There's no use in *not* listening—he's just too stubborn. Plus, he's almost always right, and this sort of mandate from him was so rare that I knew it warranted attention. When push comes to shove, sometimes you have to shove. My dad lovingly shoved me into therapy.

At first, like many people who need help, I was defensive. Psychiatric help can feel scary and unnecessarily extreme. Up until this point, the last time I'd spoken to a mental health professional was shortly after my mom died, and I hated how the "talking doctor," as we called him, would watch me play with toys and ask me questions, and then tell my dad everything I had said, like a tattletale. But despite my pushback against seeing a doctor, my dad and brother were persistent, and any time I spoke with either one of them, they demanded I get help. I am stubborn, but in my heart I always trust my family. So finally I relented and told them that I'd try. All my dad has ever asked of me is that I try.

The first thing I did was to reach out to a life coach in South Carolina named Gayle. Jeremy's family knew Gayle, and she seemed like a good fit. In my mind it felt better to work with a life coach than a "talking doctor." But a life coach is not a trained professional doctor who can handle someone who is sick. A life coach is helpful for people who are swerving within their lane, not for people who have veered off the road entirely.

Gayle told me things like "Love yourself!," but I didn't know how to love myself. She told me to get away. Go anywhere! The beach! A vacation! This turned out not to be what I needed. When you are depressed and spinning out, escaping is not the answer. You don't need to get away, you need to stay put. But instead I listened to Gayle. Jeremy and I tried to go to the Oregon coast one weekend, but he got frustrated and chastised me the entire drive there for not being happy. He didn't understand that depression was not a choice—he said he missed the old me and asked if I could just be myself again, otherwise he wasn't sure he could keep being with me. It was an impossible demand, and it broke my heart. I would spend sleepless nights whispering incessantly to myself, "I want to die," over and over—and sometimes I'd say it loud enough to wake Jeremy up because I so desperately wanted help. I once broke his computer by taking a paper clip and carving out the charging port because I could not get him to pay attention to me over his video games. I needed support from the person closest to me. But all Jeremy did was yell at me for keeping him awake, telling me this wasn't fair to him. *Fair,* what a word. The truth is that there is no fair or unfair in depression. There is just a person whose life is at stake. If I could have saved my life alone, I would have. I hoped to be able to lean on Jeremy during that time, but he was not emotionally mature enough yet to be there for me.

To someone who is clinically depressed, being told to "just be yourself again" or being reminded that "your life is really good" is very difficult and counterproductive. Hearing those things made me feel worse; it made me feel spoiled and damaged beyond repair because I could not force myself to appreciate the good things in my life, and just *be myself* again. It's hard to have gratitude when

143

you're depressed. Plus, Jeremy didn't consider that maybe I was never going to be the same person I was before, and that it was okay and even good to change. Humans are supposed to change. The process might be painful, but it is natural and necessary. On the Oregon coast with Jeremy, all I wanted to do was jump off the jagged cliffs and disappear in the ocean. I thought everything and everyone would be better off that way. To be suicidal is to live in a perpetual "grass is greener" state of mind, where you're convinced by the illusion that everything you are not is better than what you are, including being alive. It feels like you can't escape it; wherever you go, there you are.

Finally, after increasing insistence from my dad and brother, I agreed to see a psychiatrist. It was clear that my situation was more serious than something I could talk through with a life coach. I tried to make an appointment but every psychiatrist seemed to be booked indefinitely. I was learning how hard it can be to get the help you need when you finally understand that you need it. At last, through a personal referral, I got an appointment with two different psychiatrists so I could make sure I found one who worked for me. The first one I met with was a stern woman who reminded me of the helicopter mom I never had. She wore a bright red pantsuit with her hair pulled back tight. She asked me very stern, detailed questions about my thoughts. She listened to my symptoms and then looked at me how a mom might look at her kids if she caught them trying to pierce their own ears, and immediately told me that she was afraid I was going to kill myself *any day now.* The horrified way she looked at me was how *I* began to look at me. When you're depressed you become like a sponge, soaking up everything around you no matter what it is.

She raised her voice. She said she'd never met someone like me—usually a good thing, except in this situation. She said I was an extremely high-risk case—she called me a *case,* not a person—and said that I needed to get on the highest dose of the strongest antidepressant as soon as possible. She wanted to put me on medication that would sedate me entirely so that I would not have the will to kill myself if my suicidal thoughts got any worse. This kind of medication also takes away your will to do anything and effectively turns you into a walking zombie. She told me I would need to find a psychologist separately, because she was a psychiatrist. She would prescribe medicine and a psychologist would focus more on talk therapy—usually, she explained, you work with both in tandem. I was daunted by the idea of navigating two different doctors, one for medication and one for therapy. I left the appointment feeling even more like a failure.

Then I met with Dr. Arpaia, who, along with my dad, saved my life. Dr. Arpaia was both a psychiatrist *and* a psychologist, specializing in cognitive behavioral therapy. He wore giant T-shirts with wild animals on them, the kind you see for sale at gas stations. He had kind eyes. He didn't raise his voice. I felt calm around him. Like with a coach, it is very important to find a doctor you believe in. I told Dr. Arpaia everything that was going on in my life. I also told him how you only get one chance at everything in life and I had messed it up. It was all my fault and I was so spoiled and stupid to think I deserved more than I was being offered, and I was especially stupid for not being grateful for what I had before and thinking I could survive in a new place. I told him that if I could only go back in time I could fix things, but since that was impossible I had accepted that I'd had a good life, but my bubble of good luck had run out and there was no way out of the mess I had created. My life would never be better than it was before, and frankly, it would be better to die now because my best days were behind me, and it's better to quit while you're ahead. I had been thinking these things in a repetitive, taunting way, like a soundtrack incessantly playing in my head. Depression isn't just sadness; it's the same ten difficult thoughts playing over and over again. There was almost a hubris to my depression, where I felt worthless but at the same time my mind assumed it could predict the future. But we can't predict the future. The only truth about the future is that we don't know what it is. Life can be better than you could ever imagine. It can be easy to forget this sometimes, especially when you are depressed. I could only see myself through a mirror that was warped and distorted—and the mirror seemed like it reflected on itself forever. It's impossible to try to look into the future this way, because no matter how hard you try, you're still right there blocking your own view.

Admitting all of this to Dr. Arpaia, still a stranger to me, was hard but also easy. It can be easier to admit embarrassing things to someone who doesn't know you. He listened quietly, much like my dad might have, and calmly explained to me that mental illness is like when you fall and get a scrape on your knee—except instead of the cut being on your knee, it's on your brain. It takes time to heal. Your brain is a body part that can get injured like any other, and it can also heal (or be managed) like any other.

Something in my mind clicked. I'm an athlete—I know how to handle recovering from an injury. Why should my depression be any different? It was an epiphany: *the brain is a body part!* I began approaching my mental healing with just as much dedication, time, and energy as I would for any other injury.

My hamstring injury started out as a sore leg that I could have fixed on my own with some rest. As the soreness got worse, my leg probably just needed a good physio or massage therapist. But eventually, the sore leg turned into a torn tendon that needed medical intervention because it could no longer heal on its own. When you tear a tendon, you need a doctor. The rest and physical therapy that *would have* healed you earlier simply isn't enough anymore. My brain was the same way. What began as post-Olympic depression could have probably been okay if I had taken some time to rest and mentally recover. When I started feeling anxiety and fear after I moved away from Eugene, a life coach could have helped me get perspective and overcome my negative thoughts. But after months of living in a perpetual state of fear and sleeplessness, I had a "tear" in my mind that needed professional help, just like the tear in my tendon. My brain was chemically altered and needed medical intervention.

I think many people make the same mistake of not taking a mental injury as seriously as they would a physical injury. This is probably because a mental injury is invisible and doesn't necessarily limit you from showing up to work or otherwise continuing your regular routine, however terrible it might feel inside.

Dr. Arpaia told me he would not put me on severe medication because he didn't want to drug me out of this. He would pair medication (mild antidepressants and pills to help me fall asleep) with intensive talk therapy. The medication was necessary to jump-start my mind into healing itself, but medication is never enough on its own—it needs to be paired with talk therapy so that as the medication helps your brain return to a normal chemical balance, you are taking advantage of that physical healing to work on emotional healing.

Dr. Arpaia also gave me one of the most valuable truths anyone has ever taught me: first your *actions* change, then your *thoughts,* then finally your *feelings*, in that specific order. I had to accept that even though I was going to therapy three times a week and had started my medication, I was still going to be sad every day for a long time. Culturally, we seem to think that feeling happy again is like a button we can press, but it's not. Anyone who has been injured knows that the first weeks or even months of physical therapy from a serious injury can *hurt.* If an athlete breaks their leg, nobody would say to them, "snap out of it" after a couple of days off. It's understood that recovery takes time and is painful. Mental health injuries are the same way. All I could do was focus on my actions: show up to therapy, do what my doctor said, and try to be patient. The most important thing was to focus on my actions. Actions change your thoughts over time, and over even more time thoughts change your feelings. The feelings are real, yes, but try to think about your feelings as if they're stuffed animals sitting in your lap while you're driving a car. There is a fear-animal, a sad-animal, a nervous-animal, and so on. It might seem like the stuffed animal is the one behind the wheel, but really *you* are the one driving the car. That is, you are the one in charge of your own actions. The stuffed animals are just along for the ride. Stuffed animals feel less scary, and they are never in charge.

With mental health, in time, you begin thinking some days, you know what, maybe I can recover from this. Then, finally, a few months later, you wake up and start feeling like yourself again.

It's sort of like when you are in a race and you feel absolutely terrible in one moment, but that doesn't mean you should stop. In a race I never rely solely on how I feel in a moment—because it will almost always be the case that I'm hurting, and it's also almost always the case that I can push through a rough patch of pain. Racing is very painful, but we are not what we feel in any single moment, and just because I'm in the hurt box now doesn't mean I won't feel better in a few more laps. Racing is about understanding that pain is a sensation but not necessarily a threat, and if you continue to put one foot in front of the other you *will* break through your rough patch.

Likewise, I now understood that my mental rough patch could be handled similarly by showing up one day at a time and putting in the work with Dr. Arpaia to get my life back on track. I needed to take myself forward with actions like you might take a crying toddler through a grocery store: You still need to get the milk even if the toddler is crying. I stopped judging or even thinking about my bleak feelings and dark thoughts. I had faith that if I focused on my actions, my feelings would get better in time. This new understanding saved my life.

* * *

I promised myself I would become dedicated to curing my depression as if it were my next Olympics. Healing my brain was even more important than healing my hamstring. This is something my dad helped me understand. He told me that taking care of my brain was the most essential thing in the world. He told me that it might be the hardest thing I ever did but that it'd be worth it. He told me to trust him and I did. He told me to promise him I'd keep showing up—as always, my dad told me to try. For the first time in my life, I prioritized self-care and maintenance over productivity and performance.

There were moments when I wanted to give up, probably ten times a day. When those moments came, I called my dad, who always picked up the phone. I cannot thank him enough for always answering the phone—no matter what. I would try to go on a run and not be able to run more than a mile without stopping to walk and to cry. Everything around me that used to make me happy—the trees, the smells, the sky—now made me sad. I felt like an *other* in a world I used to know and love. During these times, I'd call my dad.

I would tell him I wanted to die almost every day. I had obsessive thoughts of wanting to die. But he knew that I was calling him because I didn't actually *want to* want to die. There is a big difference. He told me "Keep going, Lex," like he always did. He said I could do anything in the world except quit. He told me to just keep going. He asked me to do it for him. This was one of the only times I've ever heard my dad cry. He told me we weren't going to lose this time, and I knew exactly what he meant.

Even if my own heart was broken, I wasn't going to break his. I would show up every day and do whatever I was told. Dr. Arpaia became my new coach. I saw him three times a week and he gave me exercises ranging from going for a walk, to breathing techniques, to visualization exercises to help me fall asleep. Any time I tried to lie down I'd inevitably start thinking about something I had done wrong and then a cascade of dreadful thoughts would overwhelm me. Dr. Arpaia told me to conjure an image that was completely disassociated from my life and fixate my mind's eye on that until sleep took me. My favorite thing to visualize was an image of myself curled up inside a walnut shell, completely cozy and protected from the outside world.

Dr. Arpaia also gave me a notebook and he'd have me

write down certain things over and over again, like when I had to write "Day by day, in every way, I'm getting better and better" one hundred times. Another day my assignment was to write "I have a body but I'm not my body, I have thoughts but I am not my thoughts, I have feelings but I am not my feelings." And another day I had to write all the things I was mad at myself for and then forgive myself, like: "I forgive you for being injured," or "I forgive you for being mean to your dad," and then finish it with "and I love you anyway."

Dr. Arpaia didn't make me feel bad if one exercise didn't resonate with me. He gave me another piece of advice: Find what's useful and focus on that. Focus only on what's useful.

This advice became particularly resonant to me when I started to have epically fantastic dreams, and then I would wake up and the real world was a nightmare. In the best dream I ever had, a famous actress appeared in my high school Spanish class and gave me a stuffed owl. When I woke up I was so happy about the dream, but then suddenly so sad in real life. The better the dreams, the worse real life felt afterward. I told Dr. Arpaia that I never wanted to wake up because my dreams were so good and real life was so bad, and he told me, fine, to start taking my dreams more seriously, then. Sure, they were dreams, but they made me happy—he told me that this was my mind's way of trying to slowly help me, and that if it was useful, to pretend my dreams were real. It was helpful to understand that anything that helped me feel good, no matter how unexpected the source, was okay. As long as it's not harmful, everything is fair game when you're trying to survive depression. It was also lovely to believe that, deep inside, by creating good dreams, I was subconsciously trying to help myself.

Slowly, I began to heal. I was sad, deeply sad, for at least six months. But you can be sad and motivated at the same time. And sure enough, the sadness began to slip away, like I was a snake shedding its skin. I focused so intently on my actions that I began to forget about my feelings. When I thought about them, I noticed they weren't as potent anymore. They were turning. I came to think of myself as a stew. I had to throw a lot of things into it and then wait a very long time. If I looked inside mid-cook, it might not appear as though anything was happening. It would have been frustrating to peek into the pot too often, which is why it was important not to evaluate myself based on how I felt on any one day. I was an accumulation of all my days, good and bad. I can never know for sure what the single most helpful thing was for me, because in the end everything blended into one stew. I just know that it worked, and in time I became well again.

* * *

And as I felt more stable and healthy internally, I was able to direct my gaze outward and begin piecing together how I'd move forward. This was a much healthier approach than what I had taken before, which was to attempt to solve my inner despair by desperately trying to control the outside world. I thought that external things were what caused my depression and by fixing those I could fix myself. But what I learned was that it was important to solve my internal problems with *internal* solutions before I could re-engage with the external world. This meant seeing myself not as an athlete, an artist, or anything but a person. So many people, myself included, become depressed because we no longer live up to the labels we've assigned to ourselves. But we are all just people, and we all deserve compassion.

* * *

Recovering from my depression was the hardest thing I've ever done. I can't emphasize that enough. During my depression, I felt embarrassed about it. Now I feel proud because I am still alive.

Even though I'm no longer depressed, I still approach my mental health just like I approach my physical health.

There's a thing that athletes do called prehab, which means doing exercises and stretches along with active recovery to prevent injury. We even sometimes see professionals like chiropractors and physical trainers just to make sure our bodies are on track. Prehab is the opposite of rehab, which is something you do *after* you're injured; it keeps you healthy. I learned that you can do prehab for mental health, too. For me that means getting enough sleep, meditating, and checking in with a therapist regularly, just like I'd check in with a physical trainer.

Dr. Arpaia says that depression is a *disease of depletion,* and the signs start subtle and small. Our nervous system is the first thing to get rocked, and since we have the most nerves in our hands, face, and stomach, those are the places we should pay attention to first. It makes sense: when I'm stressed, I usually get a pimple or rash, meanwhile others might get an eye twitch or feel uncomfortable belly symptoms. When I think back to the very first days of my post-Olympic anxiety, I remember getting a canker sore that I completely ignored. As part of my new approach to staying healthy, I will pause whenever I notice something that is off about my face. For me, a pimple is very unusual. For someone else, pimples might be totally normal but stomachaches are a red flag. It might seem silly to take a day off of hard training or other work because of something as small as a pimple, but it's better to take one day off now rather than six months off later.

I've also started using a technique where, when I feel my mind start to rev up and anxiety or pre-depressive thoughts kick in, I pause and ask myself: Are my *basics* covered? By basics, I mean: Have I slept enough? Have I eaten a good meal recently? Have I gone on a run? For a friend of mine, her basics are: Are my nails painted? Did I sleep? Did I do my skin care routine? Often, I'll find that one or more of my basics have not been taken care of, and if I focus on fixing that, my negative feelings will go away. And if my basics *are* covered and I still feel bad, I know it's time to reach out for help.

Just know that however sad or depressed you might feel, you *can* get better. It's a fact. It doesn't happen all at once—it starts with sporadic moments of hope in a sea of gloom. Then there will be whole days when you don't have one bad thought, and eventually your good days will outnumber your bad days and you'll realize that you are happy. I know from experience. Recovery was a struggle, but I don't have regrets, I have tools. I now understand that falling down does not mean staying down. When I felt my happiness return, I knew that I would never again be afraid to fail.

I used to think I had to be some kind of superhero who never needed help. Now I know that asking for help is the greatest superpower in the world.

Bravey Notes

- It's normal to feel a depletion or "dip" after a big peak in life—whether it's finishing a big test, graduating from school or ending summer camp, or running in the Olympics.

- The brain is a body part and can get injured just like any body part. Mental health injuries can heal just like any other injury with professional help and enough time.

- Actions change first, then thoughts, then feelings, in that order.

- The only truth about the future is that we don't know what it will be.

girl: u ever get sad

wildflower: why

girl: u only bloom for a few weeks out of the year

wildflower: doesn't make me sad

girl: how come

wildflower: all the other weeks matter too

girl: how

wildflower: im resting, preparing, growing, becoming...

girl: oh!

wildflower: im here all year even if u can't see me

girl: forever wildflower

GLOP

Growth spurts are what it's called when a person (usually a kid) suddenly becomes much taller in a relatively short amount of time. It's as if the body builds up all its energy and then bursts upward like a coiled spring that's been released, rocketing toward the sky. Growth spurts are exciting; even the word *spurt* feels fun and quirky and energetic.

But growth spurts often come with a side effect: *growing pains.* Growing pains are what happens when a person's bones grow so fast that the skin can't keep up, and so there's an awful pain that can happen for days or even weeks at a time where your skin feels like it's being pulled apart from the inside out. I remember in first grade, I had growing pains in my shins that were so bad I couldn't walk for an entire day. I had to stay home from school, and all I could manage to do was lie in bed and let my body grow.

Growing pains aren't always physical, though. Sometimes things happen that make us grow up in an emotional way, and these experiences can leave us feeling sad, confused, angry, depressed, or any combination of tough emotions. I'm talking about experiences in life that make a lasting impression on you, where afterward you are not the same as before. Experiences like moving to an unfamiliar new town or having your heart broken or losing a loved one, or even things like coming back home after an amazing summer away at camp or moving up from middle school to high school.

These are all experiences that happen outside of our control, and sometimes it takes our hearts a little while to catch up, to grow and mature and evolve. And while we're in that catching-up phase, it *hurts*. And that's okay.

Growing pains can feel bad, but that doesn't mean they *are* bad. We can be patient with growing pain—whether it's physical, emotional, mental or all three—and even celebrate the pain because it means there are good things ahead.

But this is so, so, SO much easier said than done. Even though we're moving forward, growing pains can make us feel like we're moving backward.

After the Rio Olympics, I went through a *very* long

period of time when I was unable to compete in running at the elite level I was accustomed to before. As it turned out, the injuries I sustained during my post-Olympic depression were so catastrophic that I needed to have major reconstructive surgery on my hamstring. And during those first few months post-surgery when I could not walk (and spent my days as a literal couch potato), I grew in ways beyond my athletics. I released a book. I acted in other peoples' movies. I started developing TV shows. But deep down, I was anxious to get back to competitive racing. I didn't see myself as evolving into something new, I saw myself as stagnant—and worse, moving backward. I was not patient with my growing pains because I didn't even realize I was growing.

I had already missed the Tokyo Olympics because of my surgery, and I was anxious to race that same year to prove I was still relevant in the running world. So even though I was still relearning how to walk, I signed up for the New York City Marathon, the last possible major marathon in the same calendar year as the Tokyo Olympics. With the surgery healing and a race on the calendar, I leapt back into training with reckless abandon.

It quickly became clear that I was way in over my head. The impending New York City Marathon race date felt unreasonable given all I had faced that year, including surgery—which, by the way, I was keeping secret from the world. I felt behind and ashamed and unprepared and stressed out. I had a severe nerve pain flare-up around my hamstring, even though there was nothing actually broken or torn anymore. This is called "referred pain"— and it was a message from my body telling me to slow down and stop training so hard and thinking so much about this marathon. The body and the mind are connected in this way.

The idea of dropping out of the New York City Marathon made me sad because I was now healthy enough to run and finish the marathon, I just couldn't reach the level of fitness required to race competitively. But how could I, a so-called elite athlete, go to a major marathon and not race with my peers? I felt completely lost, like I no longer had a place in a world that I loved so much.

I called my therapist, Dr. Arpaia, and told him I was a "hot mess." I was healing but still in pain, my plan to race a major marathon in the same year as the Tokyo Olympics was unraveling, and I was completely unsure what my life was going to look like for the next few months. Dr. Arpaia understood how I was feeling, but he told me to stop thinking of myself as a mess. He said that this was an inaccurate and unfair way to identify myself. The labels we assign ourselves matter; they have a gravitational pull toward themselves.

Then he imparted upon me one of the most life-changing, useful metaphors I've ever learned: the lesson of glop. Dr. Arpaia asked me, calmly as always, if I knew how a caterpillar transforms into a butterfly. I'm no expert, but I told him that a caterpillar makes a cocoon, goes inside, then sprouts wings and becomes a butterfly. But that isn't exactly right. Dr. Arpaia explained that a caterpillar doesn't just sprout wings when it goes inside its cocoon (*chrysalis* is the more scientific term), it completely liquefies into primordial ooze—into "glop," as he described it—and then grows into a butterfly from scratch. In order to become a butterfly, the entire caterpillar must first become glop.

So in this moment where I was growing and changing into my post-surgery self, I was not a "hot mess," I was *glop.* I was transforming into a butterfly. And this period of time when I was in pain and not allowed to do anything and completely thrown out of my routine was my "glop state."

Learning about glop was life changing, because rather than seeing myself as a mess, I could see my state of disarray as a necessary step to evolving into a butterfly. Instead of moping around the house, sad about my injury, I began to march around the house triumphantly declaring that I was GLOP! I simultaneously felt pain and joy. I was amused by the process. I was going through what all caterpillars go through. The metaphor allowed me to release the pressure valve and just let myself be a blob morphing and transforming into something I couldn't predict or know ahead of time. A caterpillar doesn't know what it will be like to be a butterfly, after all.

But there's a big difference between human glop and caterpillar glop, which is that caterpillars are unconscious during their glop state, while humans are not. We are fully awake to feel the pain and uncertainty of glophood. I was certainly in pain. Pain is bad sometimes, but other times it is a really valuable catalyst for pausing, for change, for rest, and ultimately, for transformation.

Transformation can start small. One day during the glop process, I woke up and center-parted my hair, something I hadn't done since I was in first grade. I liked it. I felt strange, because for my whole adult life people had identified me as the girl with the high top bun, and suddenly I wanted a low center part. I took time to do things I never normally did, like spend an entire day alone in my house, cooking and listening to music.

But how could I be sure that I was making good decisions and transforming in a healthy way? That's another big difference between human glop and caterpillar glop: humans can decide to go back to being their caterpillar selves, while caterpillars have no choice but to become a butterfly. If I didn't embrace this time of change as a good and healthy thing, I might try to re-create everything I'd had before and everything I was before. People do this so often, stay one way forever and maintain an identity that might be holding them back, because change is scary and often painful. It is easy to hold on to what you know even if it's uncomfortable, because familiarity is inherently comforting. But humans are meant to change. That's what growth is. It's brave to grow.

* * *

Once I embraced glop-hood, little by little, my body healed. And now that I understood glop, I was no longer ashamed of my hamstring surgery, which I had kept secret from the world. My scar was not something I needed to erase, it was part of my evolution. I wanted to celebrate glop. I hired my favorite hair and makeup artist in Los Angeles to bring over her "glitter bible," a book full of dozens of pages lined with little sachets filled with different colors, sizes, and shapes of glitter. She had stars, she had hearts, she had dust-sized glitter and ant-sized glitter and everything in between. She bedazzled my surgery scar—a thick raised line that sat just beneath my right butt cheek and spanned the entire width of my leg—with the glitter. It looked like how freeways look when you see them from an airplane that is about to land at night. My talented photographer friend came over and captured photos of my scar that I shared with the world.

I had come to terms with my past, but now I needed to figure out my future. I had a big decision to make: I was still signed up to run the New York City Marathon, and even though I felt like a changed person inside, I also felt caterpillar-thoughts telling me to drop out of the race before it began and save myself the embarrassment of running a "slow" time. A *caterpillar-thought* is a thought that may be applied to our caterpillar-selves but is no longer valid or useful after we become a butterfly. Being aware of caterpillar-thoughts is the best way to evolve past them.

Usually, if an elite athlete is in a position where they aren't ready to race hard, they back out of the race and keep training until they're ready to run fast. But I really *wanted* to go to New York and run. I didn't even feel the need to race; I just wanted to go out and run a marathon. It felt expansive.

I called the marathon and told them that my body was not ready to race, and I asked if maybe I could run with the non-elites and just blend into the community. This is an important distinction, because in the NYC Marathon, the elite women start thirty minutes ahead of everyone else. The race organizers told me I still needed to start with the elites, but then I could slow down and run whatever pace

I wanted. This sounds cool in theory, but what it means in practice is that the race would start, the elite women would leave me in their dust, and I'd be running entirely alone until the main pack of runners caught up with me.

It's one thing to run a slower marathon time than normal; it's another thing entirely to do it all alone in front of thousands of people. What would everyone think of me? I almost decided to give up my spot, but then I realized: that would be a total caterpillar move. My butterfly-self wanted to be at that race. If I asked myself to think like a butterfly, then running alone didn't have to be shameful at all—it could be a celebration of health and joy. I knew there would probably be haters who'd look down on me for running slower than my peers, so if I did this, I'd have to really go into full-on butterfly mode.

And I did. I went all-out. I hired a makeup artist in New York City to come to my hotel and paint glitter on my face the night before the race, so that it would be clear to me and everyone else that I was there to have fun. I also sought out support from my wolfpack. *Wolfpack* is a term Dr. Arpaia uses to encompass the people who support you, even when you wish you could move forward confidently without outside support. I remember him telling me that wolves in the wild, who notoriously travel in packs and who could kill each other if they wanted, give each other constant nuzzles and kisses to remind each other that they're safe and supported. This is the kind of support we should seek from those closest to us. Asking for reassurance does not make us self-conscious, it makes us stronger. If wolves do it, so can we.

When the starter gun went off, I found it hard not to chase the pack of elite women in the front. I tucked into the back of their pack, but I quickly knew that this was not a sustainable pace for me. Still, I didn't know how to slow down. It can be really hard to just *slow down* in a race with all the cheering people surrounding you. I felt like I was trapped in caterpillar mode, despite my best efforts to become a butterfly. I needed a different way to approach the race.

As our first major intersection approached, crowded with hundreds of spectators, I suddenly felt the urge to dance. I can't exactly explain where the urge came from, and a caterpillar-me would never have had the nerve to do anything but run in a straight line, but deep inside, I wanted to dance. And so I did. My running stride turned into a graceful leap, like a ballerina, and it felt amazing. It also felt crazy.

The impulse to leap and dance came from deep within my nature. I knew that this gut desire to dance definitely did not come from my dad, it came from my mom. She was theatrical and flamboyant; my dad is not. For a moment, I was afraid: I resembled someone I didn't even really know. Wasn't being like my mom bad? But then I realized I was safe. I was more than safe. I was soaring. I was getting to know myself by letting me be myself. I have always wanted to know more about my mom, but in that moment, I realized that the best way to get to know my mom will always be to get to know myself.

The crowd went wild. I loved it. I danced through the entire marathon like a magical fairy. I am not a great dancer, but I did what felt good. I blew kisses, I hugged random people in the crowd, I leapt, I twirled, and it was the most joyful race experience I've ever had, right up there with the Olympics. I had gone through glophood and now I was a butterfly, and I was never going back.

The craziest thing is that my body, which had been in such severe pain, now felt agile, fluid, and free. And this wasn't just because I had taken time off to rest and recover. It was because I was finally being true to myself. Don't get me wrong, I love competing. But sports can evolve with you, people are meant to change, and I wanted to wear glitter and dance. I never thought that dancing and wearing glitter would be embraced in a marathon, especially by an elite athlete, and that made me deeply uneasy. Mental unease can thwart the body's ability to recover, which leads to physical pain, most often in the areas where we are already weakest. I was weakest in the area around my hamstring. My pain was not just from over-training after surgery; my pain was also caused by the stress in my mind.

I never used to particularly care about butterflies. They had no meaning for me. But now I love them, because I am one of them. And this brings me to the last big difference between humans and caterpillars: unlike caterpillars, who transform only once, there's no limit to how many times we humans can become glop and then evolve into a whole new creature. Glop may seem scary at first, but glop isn't bad. Glop is good.

Bravey Notes

- Growth can feel disorienting or even painful—and that's okay. Try to celebrate the discomfort as a sign that you are evolving.

- Mental stress and unease can inhibit the body's recovery and cause physical pain.

- It is easy to hold on to what you know because familiarity is inherently comforting. But humans are meant to change. That's what growth is. It's brave to grow.

what if all tears were glitter?

WILLPOWER

Looking at my life from the outside, it's clear that I do many things at once: I run, I write, I act, and I take care of my pet pug. But what isn't as obvious is all the things I'm *not* doing. For example, even if you can't tell from my social media feed, I rarely do much creative work on the days I have hard workouts. I can do many things, but not all at once—I know and respect that on workout days, my body and mind are tired and just need to rest. I am kind to myself in this way.

I wasn't always kind to myself, though. I used to think that I always needed to be pushing myself harder, further, doing more, and I'd get frustrated and upset if I felt like I was underperforming in any situation. I did not understand that I could be kind to myself and still want more out of myself at the same time.

But then I learned about *willpower*. You know how your body runs out of energy at the end of the day and you need to sleep to replenish your energy? Or if you haven't eaten in a long time, it makes sense that you need to have a meal? Well there's another reservoir in our bodies that can get depleted and refilled—and it's called *willpower*. But unlike sleep or hunger, willpower lives inside our mind. It's the mental energy that helps us make decisions, govern our actions, and handle challenges. Willpower is what helps us keep calm when someone is bothering us, and it's what allows us to say no to the temptation of looking at our social media while doing homework. It's also what allows us to simply feel like we can step out the door on a wild-weathered day and *handle it*. When my willpower is low, I make less constructive decisions than those I might make when my willpower is high. The same homework assignment might take me twice as long when my willpower is low. Our willpower on any given day is measurable and finite, which means it can be depleted, but it can also be replenished.

We make thousands of choices every day, and each of those choices uses up some portion of our willpower. The little decisions—when to wake up, what to eat, what to wear, when to leave the house—are small paper cuts that deplete willpower that *could have* gone toward bigger decisions: Should I study for that test or watch TV?

Can I finish this run or should I give up? We need to be conscious of what decisions we're allowing to use up our limited supply of willpower. Once I started becoming conscious of my own willpower, and then protective of it, two things began to happen: I became kinder to myself when my willpower was low, and I realized how many little things drained my willpower every day.

When I thought about chasing my goals and dreams, I wanted to make sure I had the willpower to give to the things that were most important to me. It's *hard* to go on a long run or sit down and write a chapter of a book. It takes concentration, discipline, and inspiration. In other words, *willpower*. If my willpower is low because I made a zillion decisions before I sit down to write, I'm more likely to get distracted or give up. So I came up with an idea called "willpower budgeting." If I only have a limited amount of willpower in a day, I want to make sure it's being spent on the things I care about most.

The best place to start is with the little things: How can you cut out some of the smaller day-to-day decisions that use up little drops of willpower? For me, having a routine and a to-do list is key. So every night, in addition to laying out my clothes for the next morning, I make sure to write out my schedule and tasks for the day ahead. I coined one of my favorite personal mantras, "Tomorrow Starts Tonight," because every small decision that I can make for myself ahead of time leaves me more willpower to dedicate to training the next morning, or to whatever big goal is on my plate.

I've also started becoming more vigilant with medium and big decisions: I am much more thoughtful about what I commit to in a single day, and I make sure that all my tasks have a set starting time and place. I am no longer down to "meet at three-ish for a run somewhere," because I understand that the back-and-forth texting leading up to the run will cost me some willpower. It's much easier to take the time to make thoughtful plans.

The best way to budget your willpower is to know yourself and understand what drains your willpower and what replenishes it. Have you ever wondered why you can stay up all night at a sleepover with friends, but doing one page of math homework makes you want to curl up into a ball and sleep? That's willpower. You might be willpower boosted by your friends but drained by your math homework. Someone else might feel the opposite, like my dad, who loves math. It's the difference between an activity that leaves you with more energy rather than less.

For example, on one of my running teams, my teammates and I used to ride together in a van to our group runs every morning. The ride was forty-five minutes long, and we usually passed the time talking. Some people love nothing more than making conversation, but I am an introvert, and I often find that socializing drains my energy. Once I started thinking about my willpower, I decided to start bringing along headphones so that when I needed to, I could remove myself from the team chit-chat. Listening to music restores my willpower—it's an activity that's *willpower boosting.* At first I felt selfish listening to music during team van rides, like I should entertain all the conversations happening around me, but now I understand that in order to chase my dreams and contribute the most to the world, I need to be protective of my willpower. I can be there for others, but I will never leave myself behind.

* * *

It isn't always easy to figure out which activities are willpower draining and which are willpower boosting, so I developed a visual tool to help me figure it out. I call it the Willpower Index. The idea for the index came about when I was recovering from an injury and had to exercise on an indoor stationary bike every day. Even though I knew that some people would *love* to spend two hours each morning biking alone in a gym, I hated it. I wanted to be running outside with my team, not stuck indoors on the bike. Then I would get mad at myself for not appreciating that I "get to bike" while other people who might love biking can't because of their full-time jobs. It was a negative feedback loop: I was upset that I had to bike, then I'd get *more* upset that I was upset. But that's not how willpower works. Willpower is different for everyone, and I was comparing my personal willpower standards to an objective standard for what I thought I *should* feel. That's where the index comes in. The Willpower Index is a simple table with an X and a Y axis. The Y axis represents a range from "bad for you" to "good for you." The X axis represents "willpower draining" to "willpower boosting."

Willpower index

good for you

willpower draining | willpower boosting

bad for you

For example, pedaling a stationary bike is "good for me" but "willpower draining," whereas for someone else, biking might be "good for me" and "willpower boosting." I understand I am biking for a good reason, but it is still draining my willpower. Staying up all night with my friends might be "bad for me" but "willpower boosting," whereas a night spent on a red-eye flight is "bad for me" and "willpower draining." Worrying about things I can't control, like obsessing about what other people think of me or being afraid that my dad might get in a car accident, is "willpower draining." Social media is an interesting one—most of us think of checking our phones as "taking a break," but is it really restoring our willpower? Most of the time, social media only serves to amplify our existing mental state, enhancing whatever it is we are already feeling: pain, longing, loneliness, you name it. An underrated willpower boosting activity for me is daydreaming: imagining wonderful things that don't yet exist (and may never exist in the real world) just for the sake of it, because it feels good.

The point is, as you budget your willpower, it's helpful to evaluate what activities are actually willpower boosting versus draining to you personally, and to maintain a balance. If my day is filled with "willpower draining" activities, then it makes sense that I feel exhausted. You wouldn't get frustrated with yourself for feeling hungry if you haven't eaten, so why get frustrated if you need to boost your willpower when it's low?

When I started understanding my willpower in this

way, not only did I have more energy to accomplish more things, but more important, I stopped beating myself up when I *didn't* have energy. That's the beauty of understanding willpower: we become kinder to ourselves.

I love cooking, but I always used to rush through it because I saw cooking as a nonproductive use of time, something to be completed as quickly as possible. But now that I understand cooking is a "willpower boosting" activity for me, I allow myself to lean in and enjoy it. I feel deserving of it. I feel a new sense of appreciation and protectiveness about my time. I understand that having fun and boosting my willpower is actually in line with achieving my goals. An interesting side effect I noticed was that I felt better about the "productive" things I *wasn't* doing.

Mastering willpower means understanding ourselves and accepting ourselves. I have a good friend with autism. Her willpower is admirable. Certain situations are willpower draining for her, and she isn't afraid to turn around and leave, midsentence if she has to, when she feels her willpower running low. In short, she does not expect herself to function beyond the boundaries of her willpower. However much she might like to do in a day, she knows that first and foremost, she must take care of herself.

In my own life, every day is a balancing act between my athletic training and any number of creative projects, business emails, and meetings. Some days I feel like Superwoman and other days I simply have to let certain things go and tell myself I am good enough for today, because I'm out of willpower. And that's okay—as long as I'm trying my best and being honest, I can forgive myself when my willpower runs dry.

Being as kind to yourself as you are hard on yourself is a skill that I've had to actively nurture. I had a college teammate named Becca who, when she felt particularly overwhelmed or otherwise dissatisfied with her day, would put on PJs, get into bed, turn off the lights, lie down for one minute, and then spring out of bed and declare "NEW DAY!," put on a new outfit, make coffee, and have breakfast again. It didn't matter if it was ten in the morning or six at night—if she sensed her day going south, she allowed herself this routine. It is the ultimate self-kindness.

Bravey Notes

- Willpower is the mental energy that helps us make decisions, govern our actions, and handle challenges. It is a finite resource that can be depleted and replenished.

- Actions, activities, and experiences that deplete and replenish *your* willpower will likely be different for someone else.

- Once you understand what drains and depletes your willpower, you can conserve and refuel it. This sustains you and also helps you to be kinder to yourself.

you can be proud of yourself
and want more out of yourself
at the same time.

MY BUGS

For two years, between kindergarten and second grade, my head was infested with lice. Yes, *two years*. I had multiple generations of the things—kids, their kids, their grandkids, great-grandkids, and more. At first it started as an itch on my head, which I told my dad about on a walk to school one day. But we were running late and he was going to miss the ferry into San Francisco and so there was no time to worry about itches. Remember, this was only his first year as a single parent. Single parents don't get sick days and neither do their kids. I only ever remember my dad letting me miss *two* days of school in my entire childhood: once in first grade when I had growing pains in my shins so bad I couldn't walk, and once during the fourth grade when he took me to opening day of the San Francisco Giants at their new stadium. Besides that, my brother and I never stayed home from school, and I think my immune system adapted to the situation because I never got sick growing up.

But this was not an ordinary childhood case of the sniffles. This was something different. I reached up and as I scratched my scalp, I felt something moving there. To my surprise, I pulled a tiny bug out from my hair. I don't remember being grossed out by it, I just remember feeling validated that I had found the source of my discomfort. I tried to show my dad, but he didn't seem to see or really register the shiny creature crawling across my finger. He was late for work and I needed to be deposited at school. I sensed this was not something he was going to fix for me, but the fact remained that I wasn't happy having bugs in my hair. So, in my five-year-old mind, I decided that the bugs in my hair were my responsibility. These were my bugs to handle.

Sometimes you ask for growth, and sometimes it is forced upon you. I felt a sudden growth spurt that I didn't ask for and didn't particularly want. When you're a kid, your entire life is guided and governed by grown-ups. They set the rules and they always know just what to do. There's a comfort in that, in knowing that somebody always has the answers. This is one of the great comforts of youth. I understood for the very first time that grown-ups *don't* always have all the answers.

As the weeks went on, I would spend my days trying to learn addition and subtraction, all the while pulling little bugs out of my hair without anyone noticing. It was very satisfying to behead the lice between my fingernails and throw them on the ground. They varied in size from roughly the dimensions of a fleck of coarse black pepper to a sesame seed all the way up to, in my memory, the size of my pinky fingernail. Sometimes my friends found bugs crawling on my shoulder. I quickly flicked them off, and most of the time, nobody thought any more about it. Kids have short memories, for the most part, except for some things that they remember forever. I thought if I could hide the evidence I would be okay.

Every day when I got home from school, I would go to the bathroom, tip my head into the sink, and shake and scratch like a crazy person. When I lifted my head back up and looked into the basin, I'd typically count anywhere from ten to forty little bugs, black shapes wriggling and exposed against the stark white porcelain. I would study them with morbid fascination, then wash them down the sink and repeat the whole process. I understood that this was a gross situation to be in, but I had also come to sort of accept it as my reality—like there might be bugs in my hair forever and this would just become another part of my daily routine, like brushing my teeth. I became a *bug-having person,* very aware that other beings were living with me all the time. *At least I'm not alone,* I would think, trying to look on the bright side. But at the same time, I knew that even if this was my new normal—I prided myself on being able to adapt to anything—this was not going to be normal to my friends or teachers or anyone else, so I guarded this secret fiercely.

Then, after carrying around my little bugs for almost two months, someone discovered my secret. A girl on the playground found a bug and asked me if it was lice. I obviously lied and told her it was just a fly. Life has always felt like a balance of wanting to stand out and fit in at the same time, but this was *not* how I wanted to stand out.

I went home and demanded that my dad help me get rid of my infestation. Private humiliation was one thing, but being called out publicly was another matter entirely. My dad has always been sensitive to being perceived as *normal,* and by now my situation was undeniably *abnormal.* By this time, we had an au pair living with us, and he passed the lice-cleaning responsibility along to her. If hair brushing and braiding fell into the category of female things, so did this.

The number of times my hair was washed with lice shampoo and mayonnaise well exceeded the norm, and none of it worked. To this day, whenever I smell mayonnaise, I think of my bugs. The full-grown lice would die in the poisonous mayo bath that the au pair rubbed into my hair, but then there were the *eggs,* which had to be meticulously combed out with a special lice pick before they hatched and the whole cycle started over. The au pair and I tried our best, but a kindergartener and a twenty-year-old aren't necessarily the most thorough combination, and between us we never got all the eggs out. I think we were both about as vigilant with the eggs as I was with coloring between the lines: we tried, but it was just too big a task.

The lice stayed so long that they outlasted the first au pair and our new one had to take over the task. Each week I'd sit patiently as she rubbed my hair full of mayonnaise and combed the bugs out. But deep down, I knew that her efforts were futile. Because the thing is, getting each and every egg out of my wild head of hair would require a surgical level of precision and commitment. And even though the au pairs meant well, ultimately I was a little embarrassed to have them do this for me. They were not my mom. I was their job, not their daughter. My au pairs would check the box of "do the lice wash," but they wouldn't necessarily sit there for hours until every last egg was gone.

By now, the lice had survived kindergarten and nearly all of first grade. I told myself I would *not* enter second grade with lice. I was almost seven years old now, older and wiser than before. The discomfort of having lice outweighed the discomfort of dealing with this issue myself. So I decided to take matters into my own hands and rid myself of lice once and for all. Carefully debugging and then de-egging myself one strand of hair at a time was something I *could* do. I figured out that the best method was to methodically pinch and drag my fingernails across each strand of hair individually so that no egg could escape unnoticed. I felt like a scientist performing an experiment on myself. After many hours of careful sorting, pinching, and threading in my bathroom laboratory, followed by a final self-administered mayonnaise bath for good measure, I was free. I had won. The lice were gone and they never came back. I felt the same sense of empowerment that I'd later feel after winning track races. Winning felt *good;* it was something I had in my control, something that couldn't be taken away from me. And then in second grade, I got my first boyfriend and I even had my first kiss. This definitely wouldn't have happened if I was too afraid to get close to anyone on account of my bugs, so I saw how my hard work paid off.

Like many things in my childhood that didn't happen in the traditional way, ridding myself of lice was ultimately my responsibility. I don't resent my dad or the au pairs for this, even though it *should not* have been my job as a first-grader to de-lice my own hair. But *should*s aren't useful to anyone, and as it turns out, I was perfectly capable of handling things myself.

It is easy and often comforting to assume there are *should*s or *supposed-to*s in the world that we can't affect or change. The au pairs were supposed to get rid of my lice. The special comb was supposed to work. The lice shampoo was supposed to kill the eggs. But it didn't. That was my reality and I could either crumble under the injustice of it or take action on my own behalf. I made the decision to get rid of *should* and take responsibility for myself. I wouldn't wish my experience with lice on anyone, but at the same time, it was thanks to my lice that I learned I could be responsible, and feeling *responsible* paves the way to feeling *capable*.

I can draw a direct line between the little girl cleaning lice eggs from her hair to the adult woman who crossed the finish line at the Olympics, made *Tracktown* and *Olympic Dreams,* and is writing this book. None of those things were supposed to happen. Dreams don't come true because they're supposed to; they come true because the dreamer takes it upon herself to make them happen. Sometimes it hurts to know you can do it.

For most dreams, there is no beaten path. If your dream is unconventional or unexpected or even impossible, then it's your challenge to tackle. There is only a thick forest of thorny blackberry bushes ahead, waiting for you to clear a path for yourself. It isn't easy. There will be blood, but there will also be berries.

Bravey Notes

- Letting go of "should" is a big step in becoming a capable and responsible person. Sometimes things will feel unfair— but unfair doesn't mean impossible.

- Dreams don't come true because they're supposed to; they come true because the dreamer takes it upon herself to make them happen.

clouds wait for no one
up in the sky
but want you to reach them
and hope you will try

SORRY

I used to say sorry a lot. Like, *a lot*. Sometimes it's good to say sorry, to take responsibility and apologize, if you have hurt someone or treated someone in a terrible way. But there is a difference between apologizing when you have truly done something wrong and saying sorry out of habit, even when you have done nothing wrong.

I used to say sorry for everything: for walking too fast, for running too slow, for eating too loud, for taking up too much space in a doorway, for playing a song I like, for basically anything that might be seen as assertive or otherwise imposing my will in other people's presence. With each *sorry,* I shrank to take up less space in the world, as if my existence was an inconvenience.

The habit got worse and worse—I was saying sorry

nearly every other sentence—until one day in college I was confronted by my friend Ben. Ben was the smartest person at Dartmouth, the valedictorian. He was very good at improv comedy and was in the group I was in. His greatest quality was his ability to be disarmingly and brilliantly honest with his scene partners. His scenes were funny because Ben was always ten times smarter than the characters he played, not just a little smarter. To watch him perform felt like watching real art; everyone felt it was special to witness his character work. But like I said, he was honest. So when Ben felt that I was saying sorry too much—like after anything I said or did—he wasn't going to keep his opinion from me.

One day, he pulled me aside and told me I was apologizing too much. That is actually a nice way of putting it. Ben was not afraid of face-to-face respectful conflict with friends—a quality I admire—so the confrontation was more of a blocking-my-path-out-of-friendly-love type of meeting. He said I needed to stop saying sorry immediately or it would be hard for him to be friends with me. He said very little else, and probably didn't need to. I was shocked, honestly used to a subtler approach from friends. But I heard him. Immediately, I began to try to drop the habit. I placed my tongue behind my front teeth anytime I felt an unnecessary sorry coming out of my mouth, such as when I took the last cookie or when I disagreed with someone on any issue, big or small. I appreciated what he told me. I followed through. I say sorry much less often today. But this interaction, for me, went beyond dropping a bad habit. This was about what Ben meant, really, by telling me to stop saying sorry.

You know what the most beautiful thing is: when a friend says something to you that, in so many words, tells you that you are enough. I don't think I saw it that way then, but I see it that way now. Ben was just trying to tell me that I didn't need to say sorry for existing; I was good enough to justify my life without punctuating it with more *sorry*s than there are needles on a cactus. I'd always thought that if someone apologized too much, it was offensive to others, like a cactus prick to the arm. But being offensive wasn't the problem. A good friend who tells you to stop saying sorry simply loves you and thinks you're great without the apology. They see the cactus skin as pointing inward . . . that is, they see you as hurting yourself, which, when you think about it, is true. Every apology you offer is you saying you don't belong on this earth as you are. I am still trying to use *sorry* less in circumstances when I am safe, when I am enough.

Bravey Notes

- It's wonderful to take responsibility and apologize when you've done something wrong, but you never need to apologize for simply existing and taking up space in the world.

the thing about scary things
like spiders
is that they do not scare me nearly as much
as the things i want the most.
the *want* things creep and stay
live in my mind —
a much harder place to reach and find
cannot be killed
will grow instead
unlike the spider in my bed
are not afraid
and will not flee
rather than b_o_o
say c_o_me _a_nd g_e_t _me_.

FOR THOSE WHO DREAM

Like a middle school crush, I think about my dreams more often than I'd like to admit. Having big dreams is awesome. I wake up every day imagining and wishing for a future that doesn't exist yet but hope might one day become real. But how does a dream become real?

All dreams are born in the imagination and exist as intangible bundles of potential until we decide to take action in the real world and make our dreams come true. What lives in our imagination is only intangible until it's not. When I was little, I felt a vast ocean of ambition within me, full of life and energy, but I wasn't old enough yet to shape that ambition into any specific goal. Instead, I felt a vague sense of wanting to be like the people I idolized most in my young life: Britney Spears, my teenage babysitters, and my favorite teachers at school. I wanted to be someone who made people feel what those people made *me* feel. And as I got older, I learned how to channel that vague ambition into specific goals.

The first step to committing to a dream is to write down your goal so that it is not just a thing floating inside your head. This way, you're holding yourself to something tangible, and when you achieve your dream you'll have the physical proof that you were brave enough to want it in the first place. You talk about it like it's real, you take it seriously, and this makes it more inevitable. This is why I named my dog Bernini before I got her. I knew I wanted a pug and talked about her like she would be real. I even bought a little collar that I kept on my desk years before I got her (though when I did get her, I learned that pugs don't wear normal collars— they wear harnesses), because it reminded me that she would be a real thing in my life. Inevitability is like momentum: it starts slowly and with difficulty, but it builds over time until it's as clear and powerful as if it always existed.

In the early stages of dream-chasing, when we first take a dream out of our imagination and think "I want to try and make this real," it is very fragile. It's like a campfire. If you've ever built a campfire, you know the feeling: you need to be extra thoughtful and careful with the first small flame and nurture it so it can take hold and grow. Dreams are delicate, and it's easy for you or others to find the million reasons why the thing from your imagination won't become real. Just like a small gust of wind can extinguish a fledgling campfire, a small negative comment can squash a dream. If someone reacts by saying *that's stupid,* the dream can die. Or if you want to try out for a sports team but think *I'll never make it,* that dream dies, too.

The best thing to do when bringing an idea to life is to create a safe environment for it to thrive. In our campfire metaphor, that means protecting the match from the wind and setting up lots of kindling. Kindling can take many forms: hanging inspirational posters on your wall, listening to inspiring interviews, wearing a superhero cape that you like, watching movies that make you feel inspired, or any other form of support from the outside world. Gather it all like you would gather kindling. In my experience, the single most powerful form of kindling comes in the form of people who encourage you and make you feel like *you can do it.*

In Hollywood, the best creative collaborators on film sets are people whose natural inclination is to build each other up rather than bring each other down. The answer is always *yes* or at least *maybe* before it's *no.* This is a good quality to look for and actively cultivate in any friendship or relationship. *Yes* people may even give you feedback or constructive criticism that will help you improve your process. Feedback can sometimes hurt, but it doesn't have to. I like to think about feedback from people I trust and admire like bloodwork: as an athlete, I periodically check my blood to see if my calcium, Vitamin D, and iron levels (among other metrics) are optimized. I test my blood levels because I always want to make sure I'm healthy and improving. Likewise, I seek out advice and feedback from trusted *yes* people to keep me on track. If my blood tests come back and show poor levels of iron, for example, there's no use feeling upset about it. I've just discovered a truth that would have been there whether I'd learned it or not. If someone I trust tells me a difficult truth about my work, I try not to take it personally, I understand the feedback is meant to help me manifest my best self, and it is also ultimately up to me whether to apply the feedback to my work.

How do you know if the feedback, commentary, or criticism you're hearing is coming from a *yes* person or a *no* person? Well, does it feel like their words are putting your fire out, or are they gently but firmly helping you grow? It's true that you blow on a flame to make it get bigger. You can also blow on a flame to extinguish it. It's all about the intention.

. It isn't always immediately obvious when someone is a *no* person—it starts small. *No* people are threatened by someone who is chasing their dreams. They prefer that the people around them remain unchanging because this makes them feel safe. Instead of encouraging you when you make an effort to chase a dream and break the mold, *no* people laugh at you as if you're cute but misguided— and then before you know it, you're living a life that doesn't reflect the grandeur of your dreams, whatever they are. Even small dreams have their grandeur.

So if you're someone who wants to *do* things, you'll come to realize that chasing a dream is hard enough without also putting yourself at the disadvantage of being with a *no* person. And if you find that you're being a *no* person to yourself—if *you're* the one putting yourself down—don't worry. The fact that you're noticing it means that it's totally within your power to change. You can always decide what kind of person you'd like to be.

It might be tempting to play it safe and never take a dream out of your head. If you aren't sure you're ready to commit to your goal, try this exercise that a mentor shared with me: Imagine that all of a sudden, pursuing your goal is not an option at all for you anymore. It has been magically taken away. How do you feel? If you feel relief, then you know it wasn't right for you. But if you feel heartbroken imagining a world where you can't chase your goal, then the decision to commit is clear.

Once you commit, give yourself a window of time to be dedicated to pursuing your goal. During this time, do not question the goal itself. You don't question the workout in the middle of a rep, right? You give it your all until the rep is done and then you reassess. It's even okay to want to change your goal, but try your best to make those decisions after you've given it a fair shot. A great coach once told me that when the pain sets in during a workout, it takes less mental energy to push harder than it does to think about slowing down or stopping. I've found that to be true: momentum matters, physically and mentally.

Chase your goal until the window of time is over and then check in with yourself. The exact duration of this window is up to you, but make sure you set a clear start and end date for it.

This leads me to the next point, and it's an important one: don't make the window of time between check-ins too long or too short. Give yourself long enough for it to feel like a commitment, but not *too* long. If you try to plan too far ahead, you might limit yourself. It's good to give yourself space to grow and evolve. If I had tried to plan, say, five years into the future after I graduated from college, I would have counted myself out of being an Olympian entirely. Instead, I only planned a year in advance, and then allowed myself the chance to outgrow my expectations and set new ones each year. The path to achieving a dream is often circuitous and hard to predict. My rule of thumb for major life dreams is to look ahead one year at a time—and in the meantime, be in the present. Honor the moment you're in. Capture your right-now truth. Your work can forever stand as proof of where you are in this moment, which is the realest thing there is. Dream-chasing is about process, not perfection.

Next, figure out what resources you actually need to enable yourself to fully chase your dream during your window of time. This means the tangibles and the intangibles. Tangibles might be things like running shoes, paintbrushes, or ballet slippers. Intangibles are things like free time, a supportive coach, or teammates.

Once you have your needs taken care of, it's time to show up and then keep showing up every single day. It's time to take your commitment seriously. It's time to do the same thing over and over. It's sometimes easy to feel like there's not enough time in the day, but time can be elastic. I used to leave my exercise equipment scattered around the house, on account of being too busy to pick up after myself, until one day I broke my pinky toe when I accidentally stubbed it on a weight I'd left in the living room. All of a sudden, I had time to go to the hospital and rehab my foot for the next few weeks. Finding the five minutes a day to tidy up my equipment became easy after that. "I don't have enough time" is not a useful excuse when it comes to anything related to your dream. It's okay to actively choose to do something or not, but don't blame time. Take responsibility.

Soon enough, things will get hard. It can be easy to forget how hard *hard* really is. The biggest misconception about chasing a dream is that every moment will feel fun. But that isn't how it works, especially in the beginning. In fact, most beginnings are more hard than fun for a very long time. It can help to remember that when you are chasing your dream, you are also *living* your dream.

When an athlete is training for the Olympics, whether they end up making the team or not, there is still that window of time where they are living the Olympic dream. The *chasing* is a part of the dream. So much of the process happens in the chasing time, when we're putting ourselves out there and going for something that we want very badly—and it's so easy to let anxiety about the outcome ruin the whole experience. So instead of only worrying about the end outcome, why not also enjoy the dream while you're in it? Even if it ends sooner than we might have hoped, we can give ourselves the gift of blissfully living the dream while it's still in our hands.

It is very easy to extinguish your own campfire and kill an amazing idea by judging it too soon. This used to happen to me all the time—I'd look at a rough draft of something I was working on and I'd fear that it would never be good. I'd become paranoid that the things I feel in my mind and heart could not translate into words anyone else could understand or feel. I'd fearfully think that my ideas weren't special, and therefore I wasn't special, and therefore I didn't belong in the world. This kind of spiraling negativity is understandable, but it's not necessary. Or useful. I remind myself that every draft seems bad before it's good, and the most important thing is to not let the fire die out. I need to keep nurturing it. Blow on the flame steadily, not too hard. Tending to your creative work means looking away and watching at the same time. You have to let it breathe. You can't control a campfire.

When you commit to chasing your dream, think of yourself like Alice from *Alice in Wonderland:* From her perspective there were times when being in Wonderland must have been quite challenging and stressful. Alice grows and shrinks, she is sentenced to death, and she literally fills a room with her tears at one point. Alice was constantly out of her comfort zone and tackling new challenges. There was work, but there was also Wonderland.

Chasing a dream means giving a hundred percent of what you have every day. This doesn't mean every day is a success. Some days, a hundred percent of what you have doesn't amount to much. That's okay as long as it really was a hundred percent of what you had that day. It isn't helpful to fixate on the end result. The only thing that's in your control is the progress you're making today. You trust that, if you keep trying, you will come to the finish line eventually, whatever the finish line looks like for you. The end result will not always be in your hands. What *is* in your hands is the *try.*

It can feel safer to think that certain things are impossible than to believe that just about anything is possible if you are scrappy, creative, and bold, and don't give up—if you see barriers as things to overcome rather than reasons to quit. Some barriers are systematic in nature, like the challenges that girls face in the distance running world when they go through puberty. Others are discriminatory based on race, sexual orientation, and a myriad of other identifiers. I recognize that I cannot speak to the difficulties of systemic barriers that I haven't faced myself. But speaking from my own experience, I believe it's best to face all barriers head-on and fight for your dreams as hard as you can, even if it seems impossible. You can either stop making excuses for yourself or you can lead a life defined by your excuses. It can be intimidating to open yourself up to this belief, and you're likely going to have to face hard questions about whether you truly want to put in the effort for something that may at first seem impossible. I say, if you want something, decisively try to get it. That beats the alternative, which is a slow-simmering regret that often reduces into bitterness. It's better to be brave than bitter.

It takes bravery to stay the course. Setbacks will happen, and likely they'll be out of your hands because you can't control the world, the future, or anybody else. But how you think about your setbacks is entirely in your control, and this is actually more important than the setback itself. For example, if you fall down on a run, instead of becoming frustrated and letting your whole practice get ruined, rewrite the narrative in your favor: you fell because you were meant to slow down and take that run easy. Other times, a setback happens and you just have to power through. When I was in college, I was walking down the streets of New York City to my first and only corporate job interview when my right high heel got stuck in a metal steam vent in the sidewalk. I tried to wriggle my foot free and the heel snapped off! I was running late and I couldn't miss the interview, so I decided to pretend that my shoe had an invisible ghost-heel attached where the actual heel used to be, effectively walking on my toes through the entire office building with my single real heel making the signature clicking sound on the marble floor every other step. I don't know if anyone noticed the heel was missing. And I don't care. It's about relentlessly staying on your own team no matter what, no matter how large or small the setback. But people who are committed must suspend their disbelief. Being committed isn't about the end result; it's about giving yourself the very best chance to get there.

When you face a setback, you have to stretch your efforts and resources more than you'd like. But even when facing a setback that seems insurmountable, committed people never see it as a dead end because that is not the story they tell themselves.

Sometimes life is simply unfair. Sometimes things happen to us or those we love that feel completely unmerited, random, unprecedented, and otherwise *unfair*. When I was eight years old I spent the entire summer making and selling lemonade along the perimeter of the island I grew up on with one of my close friends, Megan, but then her older brother stole the entire $63 of our hard-earned money at the end of the summer. I could not believe it. I felt so upset, because her parents didn't do anything about it, and I didn't even want to tell my dad because I knew he wouldn't do anything about it. It felt like a completely up-ending emotional tsunami—I was beside myself, because it never crossed my mind that someone would actually steal all the money and get away with it. It showed me that my entire reality could be altered in an instant and also that life is not always fair. It is helpful to accept that these random misfortunes will randomly occur, but we need not read too much into them. Think about them like a rainstorm. We don't *deserve* to have a rainstorm come and wash away our chalk art; it just happens sometimes. Unfairness is as random as a rainstorm. We can carry a raincoat around with us, but if we happen to get soaking wet, we will dry, eventually. We might even find reason to dance in the rain, if we understand that rain isn't personal. You're going to be fine and you deserve to be fine.

We all have stories in our heads that can help us or limit us; make sure you understand what story you're telling yourself. People who are not committed are often tempted to tell themselves the story that it was just too hard to achieve this particular goal, that they didn't get a fair chance, or any number of legitimate-seeming narratives leading to a false inevitability. It's easy to compare yourself to other people and decide that they have it easier than you for one reason or another, or they have more talent than you, and label *that* as the reason you can't succeed. But the thing is, no one chases their goal from a level playing field. It's important to stay on your own team and to understand that there are countless paths to achieving the same goal. Just because someone else appears to be in the lead early in a race doesn't mean they'll finish first. The most important thing is that *you* are thriving on your own path. Chasing your dream is hard enough; you don't need your own mind weighing you down with tempting excuses to quit. Remember, your narrative is entirely subjective and completely up to you.

Sometimes a setback shows you that you need to make a change in your approach or rethink your time frame and pivot your goals. That's okay—it's all part of the learning process. Try not to beat yourself up. The only real mistake is knowing you need a change and not making it. It's only a mistake if you don't fix it. If something doesn't go your way, call it a *lesson* and adjust accordingly. Last but not least, understand that a dream comes true very slowly and then all at once. Most of the time you will be in that "very slowly" period. Don't let people make you feel dumb or naïve during this time. Hopefully your commitment to your goals will inspire people rather than intimidate them, but it is also true that when you try hard, it might make some people uncomfortable, and that's okay. Just remember that their feelings are not about you. Still, it's easy for people to make us dream-chasers feel self-conscious and silly, at least early on. Remember, chasing a dream goes against most peoples' instinct, which is to seek out safety at all costs. To them, chasing dreams is a waste of time.

But contrary to what some people might say, *chasing a dream is not a waste of time.* It's only a waste of time if you're doing it halfway. It's possible that you will not succeed. But then again, maybe you will.

Maybe—that word is bursting with possibility. *Maybe* is a blank canvas that you can paint with inevitability if you are committed. It is often unglamorous, at least from the outside. But it's brave to be committed. You are replacing *can't* with *maybe.* You are manifesting the greatest expression of yourself. You are fulfilling your destiny. You are being a Bravey.

Bravey is a book about chasing dreams, and what I want to say here is that there is only so much time we have on earth, and we should chase after those dreams with all the exuberance and energy of a kid running after an ice cream truck. The time will never be enough and it also must be enough.

The most amazing thing is when a dream has fully left your imagination behind and become an actual thing in the world that other people can interact with. Like when I am making a movie and I see actors reading lines that I wrote. Maybe an architect feels the same way when one of their buildings gets built, or a chef when a dish they dreamed up comes out of the oven for the first time. It's the same as watching a roaring campfire and knowing that it used to exist only as a small match in my pocket and a tiny pile of kindling. It's the closest thing I can think of to magic.

Bravey Notes

- A dream starts out as something that lives inside your imagination, but dreams can become real by taking certain specific steps, including writing your goal down, avoiding "no" energy, committing for a set period of time, knowing what you need and what you don't, focusing on trying your best rather than being the best, and understanding that setbacks are a part of chasing a dream.

- The result is not in your hands. What *is* in your hands is the "try."

i want to be brave like the first time
& wise like the last time
all at once.

THE END OF
THE BEGINNING

When my papou passed away, I remember watching my dad say goodbye to his father and I saw this look in my dad's eyes that reminded me of me. There was sadness, but not a terrible sadness—my grandpa was more than ninety years old and had been sick for some time—it was a *yearning* sort of sadness. It was sadness from a place of gratitude, like he wished he could tell his father "thank you" one more time.

After the funeral, my dad and I were in a hotel room together and I was trying to tell him in the last few moments before I needed to catch a cab to the airport that I hoped he would take better care of himself. He'd been neglecting his fitness and I wanted to tell him that he wasn't immune to the physical degeneration that my papou had faced. I expressed concern that my dad had just spent months and months managing his father's health issues, and before that he spent years raising my brother and me, and before that he spent I don't know how long trying to keep my mom alive. And now, finally, I needed to tell him to his face to please take care of himself and go to the gym three times a week.

And my dad just smiled at me with a larger than normal smile and I was perplexed—here I was chastising him and all he did was smile. It was almost farcical. I became frustrated, wondering if my dad wasn't taking me seriously or if he was just truly impenetrable. But then I realized he wasn't smiling because he was laughing at me; he was smiling because he was *proud* of me. He was so proud that I was mature and stable enough to care about him in this way. It meant that I was responsible enough for myself to also feel responsible for somebody else. He was smiling because now, in this moment, he knew that I was going to be okay.

When I was of the tucking-in age and my dad used to tell me every night "You're a good kid, you know that," I think what he was really saying is that while this wasn't exactly how he planned on raising me, he was doing his best and hopefully it was all amounting to something good. As if calling me a good kid every night would make me into a good kid. I have to assume it helped, because I am here as a product of all the things, including those good-night somethings, that my dad did for me.

And he really did so much for me. I can't even imagine how my dad felt about me after my mom died—how could he ever think I'd turn out okay after that? Surely not unless he dedicated his entire life to me, which he did. I imagine that he might have felt like a grown man in a dollhouse, or the only human on a desert island with a little alien who never stopped crying and laughing and demanding things from him. Everything in his life came second to taking care of my brother and me. He felt we needed him more than he needed himself. It makes me feel so spoiled and thankful all at once. I have tried to thank him, often imperfectly, like the time I was so motivated to be a good kid in fourth grade that I accidentally polished our wood floors with table polish, rendering all the floors in our house slippery as ice. I like to think he appreciated my effort, even if he did fall down the stairs.

My dad is an engineer, and he always preferred to teach me life lessons through actions rather than words. He taught me how to throw a baseball before he taught me how to write, which is why he gave me my brother's right-handed glove before he learned I was left-handed. Sports were the best language for him to teach me how to explore "good pain," how to work hard and push myself to the limits of my body and mind without actually hurting myself, without going to the "bad pain" place.

Success as an athlete was always the best way to show my dad that I was going to be okay. Every race I competed in was my way of showing him—and myself—that we were *doing it*. We were surviving and thriving despite and maybe because of our tragic past. The Olympics were for my dad as much as they were for me.

Truthfully, running has always been a way for me to matter, which has been the most essential mandate in my life after my mom left me in the way that she did. Performing as a runner or as an actor—any kind of performance—is a way to matter. The thing about mattering in this way, though, is that it makes me feel fulfilled and lonely all at once. If the only way I can matter is by performing, then it means that my self-worth is coming from outside rather than within. If there's nobody in the audience, do I matter?

I used to think that my professional achievements might be able to satisfy the *want* that I feel, as if external accomplishments and praise would finally give me the sense of mattering that I so desperately craved. I admit that deep inside, I will always have that want. But now I understand that no matter what I do, *I matter*. I matter in this world simply because I am in this world. I am still chasing my dreams with the reckless abandon of a kid chasing an ice cream truck, but underneath it all, I understand that I am here and that is enough.

I also understand I am always going to be growing up. It is not done. It will never be done. I will always keep learning and discovering new things. When I make mistakes, I will be less unkind to the yesterday-me, who didn't know better. My younger selves will always be contained inside me, watching me grow up and occasionally trying to offer commentary and wisdom that may or may not be useful. Sometimes my younger selves take control and I act immature or otherwise misbehave in ways I'm not proud of. In those moments, I will be kind to the today-me, who is just trying her best. I will also remember that the person I am meant to be may not exist yet.

I am okay. I am never going to end up like my mom. There were times when both my dad and I weren't sure. But now I'm sure. And I'm sure he's sure. *I am okay.* We did it. And so my dad's goofy smile in the hotel room after Papou's funeral made me cry because it is only someone who has had serious fears, probably about himself as a dad more than about me as a daughter, who could smile in *that way.* Only people who were once nervous and uncertain can feel this kind of relief, joy, and pride. We are where we are thanks to everything that happened, and where we are is good.

Many things behind
many things ahead
why feel afraid
when you can be brave instead?

ACKNOWLEDGMENTS

Thank you to my family and friends.

Thank you to Eliza Rothstein and the Inkwell team.

Thank you to Beverly Horowitz and the Random House team.

Thank you Maya Hawke.

Thank you to Mommy, who has her copy in the sky.

Thank you to the Braveys.

ABOUT THE AUTHOR

Alexi Pappas is an award-winning writer, filmmaker, and Olympic athlete. Her writing has appeared in the *New York Times, Runner's World, Women's Running, Sports Illustrated,* the *Atlantic,* and *Outside,* among other publications, and she has been profiled in the *New York Times, Sports Illustrated, New York,* and *Rolling Stone.* Pappas cowrote, codirected, and starred in the feature film *Tracktown* with Rachel Dratch and Andy Buckley. She cowrote and starred alongside Nick Kroll in *Olympic Dreams,* the first non-documentary-style movie ever to be filmed at the Olympic Games. Alexi most recently directed and starred in the feature film *Not an Artist* alongside RZA, Ciara Bravo, Paul Lieberstein, Matt Walsh, and Haley Joel Osment. A Greek American, Pappas holds the Greek national record in the 10,000 meters and competed for Greece in the 2016 Olympics. She lives in Los Angeles.

alexipappas.com

@alexipappas

@alexipappas

askbravey@gmail.com

Olympic athlete, actress, filmmaker, and writer
Alexi Pappas shares what she's learned about confidence,
self-reliance, mental health, embracing pain, and achieving
your dreams, in her debut memoir for adults.

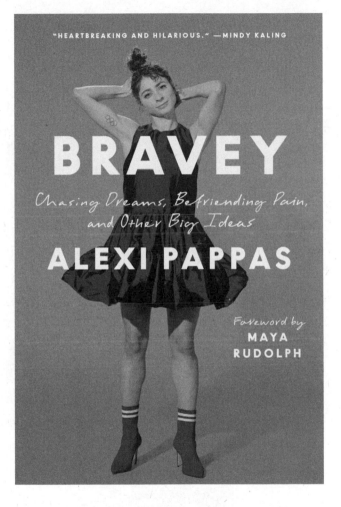

"Alexi's heartbreaking and hilarious book inspired even
me to want to put on some sneakers and run."

—MINDY KALING